Building a Cybersecurity Culture

A Strategic Guide to Protecting Your Business

by

Andy Wood

Copyright 2024 Andy Wood. All rights reserved.

No part of this book may be reproduced in any form or by any electronic or mechanical means, including information storage and retrieval systems, without permission in writing from the author. The only exception is by a reviewer, who may quote short excerpts in a review.

Although the author has made every effort to ensure that the information in this book was correct at press time, the author does not assume and hereby disclaim any liability to any party for any loss, damage, or disruption caused by errors or omissions, whether such errors or omissions result from negligence, accident, or any other cause.

This publication is designed to provide accurate and authoritative information about the subject matter covered. It is sold with the understanding that the publisher does not render professional services. If legal advice or other expert assistance is required, the services of a competent professional should be sought.

The fact that an organisation or website is referred to in this work as a citation and/or a potential source of further information does not mean that the author endorses the information the organisation or website may provide or recommendations it may make.

Please remember that Internet websites listed in this work may have changed or disappeared between when this work was written and when it was read.

Acknowledgements

Writing this book has been an incredible journey, and I am grateful to all who have supported me – colleagues, family and friends.

I want to thank my wife, Sally, for inspiring me to write this book. Her constant encouragement and belief in my ability to write this book have been a true source of inspiration. Her unwavering support and motivation have pushed me to strive for excellence in everything I do.

Finally, to the readers of this book: thank you for investing your time in the crucial task of building a security-conscious culture. I hope this guide provides the tools and inspiration to drive meaningful change within your organisations.

With sincere gratitude,

Contents

Preface 1

Introduction 3

Chapter 1: Security Transcends Technology 5
    Why a Cultural Shift is Essential for Enhanced Security 6

Chapter 2: The Threat Landscape 11
    Modern Security Threats: An Overview 12
    The Impact of Technology on Security 19
    Behavioural Insights into Security Risks 28
    How Bad Can It Get When It Goes Wrong? 37

Chapter 3: Foundations of a Security Culture 41
    Principles of a Resilient Security Culture 43
    Strategies for Mindset Change 46
    Leadership in Security Culture 57

Chapter 4: Introducing Behavioural Science 67
    Introduction to Behavioural Models and Theories 69
    Modern Research and Emerging Trends in Behavioural Science 74
    Applying Behavioural Science to Change Security Behaviours 78
    Designing Interventions That Stick 82
    Technology as an Enabler 86
    Measuring Cultural Impact on Security 93

Chapter 5: The Seven Dimensions of Security Culture 103
    Behaviour 106
    Attitudes 112

Cognition 121

Communication...129

Compliance..140

Norms...151

Responsibilities 162

Building a Strong Security Culture 168

Chapter 6: The Global Organisation 171

Cultural Diversity in Security Practices 173

Chapter 7: Psychological Safety 193

The Benefits of a Trust-Based Approach 195

Implementing a Cyber Psychological Safety Policy 196

Chapter 8: Security Champions 199

The Role and Importance of Security Champions 201

Identifying and Selecting Security Champions.............................205

Training and Resources for Security Champions.........................209

Strategies for Champion Engagement..213

Chapter 9: Future Proofing Security 219

Anticipating Future Threats...220

Scalable and Adaptable Security Strategies 224

Chapter 10: Integrating Culture Change into Strategy 229

Evaluating the Current Cultural Landscape...................................231

Cultural Barriers and Facilitators 236

Principles of Culturally Aware Security Strategies.......................240

Behavioural Insights to Shape Security Behaviours....................243

Measuring Cultural Improvements 247

Refine Strategies With Feedback Loops 251

Examples of Good Cyberculture Programmes 255

Chapter 11: Key Insights and Future Trends 263

Summary of Key Insights 265

Future Trends 268

A Final Word 273

Cybersecurity culture (aka Cyberculture) refers to the shared *attitudes*, *behaviours*, *knowledge*, and *actions* characterising an organisation or community's approach to cybersecurity. It encompasses how people within the organisation perceive, understand, and respond to cyber threats and security protocols. A robust cybersecurity culture promotes *awareness*, *vigilance*, and *proactive behaviours* to protect digital assets and information.

Preface

Reflecting on my transition from the structured world of Information Technology to the dynamic realm of cybersecurity, I've realised a profound transformation in my understanding of effective security. In the early stages of my career, I firmly believed that technology held the key to good security. It was a time when I saw the world through the lens of firewalls, anti-virus, and encryption, convinced that the right combination of technological tools could safeguard the most vulnerable data.

However, as years passed and cyber threats became more complex and sophisticated, it became clear that even advanced technology was always a step behind cyber adversaries' ingenuity. This relentless cycle of attack and defence illuminated a crucial realisation: security transcends technology, demanding a shift from reactive protocols to proactive resilience.

This book delves into how security, far beyond the confines of technology, becomes a cornerstone of modern business strategy. It focuses on developing an ethos that must permeate every layer of an organisation. It's a journey highlighting how fostering a culture of security awareness and responsibility can fortify businesses against the ever-evolving landscape of cyber threats.

Most importantly, the narrative illustrates the realism that security is not the sole responsibility of the Security or IT departments but a shared organisational value. It also argues for a shift in perspective - viewing security not as a cost centre but as a strategic asset that underpins trust, resilience, and innovation.

Welcome to the future of security, where culture transcends technology and security champions lead the way. I hope you find this book a valuable resource for creating an effective strategy to deliver a security-conscious culture within your organisation. By embracing cultural transformation and behavioural insights, organisations can build resilient security cultures that stand the test of time.

Introduction

In today's interconnected world, where cyber threats are evolving at an alarming pace, the ability to protect an organisation no longer rests solely on technology. Instead, the real strength lies in building a security-conscious culture that weaves security awareness into the very fabric of business operations. Modern businesses face unprecedented challenges, and resilience against these threats demands more than reactive measures. It requires a proactive approach grounded in both cultural change and behavioural insights.

This book explores how businesses can develop a strong security culture, not just as a safeguard but as a strategic advantage. By understanding and influencing human behaviour, leaders can inspire a shift in mindset across the organisation, transforming security from an afterthought into a shared responsibility.

Creating this cultural shift means moving beyond traditional security practices. It involves equipping employees with the knowledge and behaviours needed to recognise, respond to, and ultimately reduce cyber risks. This requires a deep understanding of behavioural change – how habits are formed, sustained, and embedded into everyday working life.

Leaders play a pivotal role in fostering this change. But it's not just about top-down directives; a resilient security culture engages everyone, from the boardroom to the frontline. The goal is to embed security-conscious behaviours at every level, creating an environment where vigilance becomes second nature.

The pages ahead offer practical insights and strategies to help businesses navigate this complex terrain. We'll explore the intersection of culture, behaviour, and security, providing guidance on cultivating a robust, adaptable organisation that can withstand today's threats and those yet to emerge.

As the cyber landscape continues to shift, the time to prioritise security culture is now. This book aims to equip you with the strategies and knowledge needed to drive meaningful change and build a future-proof business in the face of modern threats.

Chapter 1

Security Transcends Technology

In today's fast-evolving digital era, the security landscape that businesses and their leaders face is shifting dramatically. This change reveals a crucial reality: the nature of security threats has evolved from primarily physical challenges to a complex mixture of cyber, physical, and cyber-physical threats.

Addressing these threats requires more than technological solutions; it necessitates a fundamental shift in the security culture. Merely installing the latest security software or enforcing strict access controls is no longer adequate. The current environment requires an approach that weaves security awareness deeply into the fabric of an organisation's culture.

This chapter highlights the urgent need for a cultural shift towards enhanced security, setting the stage for a deeper examination of modern security threats, their impact on businesses, and the role of human factors in security vulnerabilities in the following chapters.

As leaders, you stand at the vanguard of this battle. Adopting the need for this cultural transformation is the first step in fortifying your organisation against the continuously evolving array of security threats.

Why a Cultural Shift is Essential for Enhanced Security

The need for a profound organisational culture transformation is more evident in the fast-evolving security landscape where traditional protective measures frequently fall short. This shift isn't just a luxury; it's an indispensable part of the arsenal against cyber and physical security vulnerabilities. The core of this transformation is to imbue every level of the organisation with a security-conscious mindset, making security a responsibility of every individual.

The significance of a cultural shift to enhance security cannot be overstated. As technology progresses, so do the methods of those with malicious intentions. The ongoing battle between evolving technologies and advancing threats demonstrates that relying solely on technological solutions is inadequate. Instead, robust security practices and a culture that actively promotes and values these practices are essential.

Consider the last major security breach you are aware of. It likely involved human error - perhaps a lost laptop, a weak password, or a phishing scam. This highlights that human error often represents the most significant vulnerability in an organisation. Changing technology or processes isn't enough; transforming people's attitudes and behaviours is crucial.

A culture that prioritises security empowers individuals to counter threats proactively. When employees adopt a security-first mindset, they become an active part of the defence mechanism, capable of identifying and mitigating risks before they materialise. This proactive stance is vital in an environment where threats can arise unpredictably and evolve rapidly.

Leadership is crucial in nurturing this culture. Leaders must exemplify the security behaviours they expect to see throughout the organisation. This responsibility extends beyond mere advocacy; it includes equipping all organisation members with the necessary resources and education. When leaders demonstrate a genuine commitment to security, it inspires everyone to follow suit.

Instilling a security-conscious culture demands sustained effort. It can't be achieved overnight, nor can it be sustained with a set-it-and-forget-it approach. Ongoing education and awareness campaigns are essential to keep security at the forefront of everyone's mind and adapt to the ever-changing threat landscape.

Another effective strategy is to encourage good security practices. By recognising and rewarding proactive security behaviours, organisations can underscore the importance of vigilance and shared responsibility, fostering a collective investment in their security posture.

Moreover, fostering an open and responsible culture is key. Employees should feel comfortable reporting potential security threats without fear of retribution. An environment that punishes mistakes can inhibit reporting security risks, rendering the organisation more vulnerable.

Tailoring cultural initiatives to align with the organisation's specific context is vital. A one-size-fits-all approach is unlikely to be effective. Security culture initiatives should be designed and implemented in consideration of cultural, sector-specific, and organisational characteristics.

Empowering employees with the knowledge and tools to protect themselves and the organisation is foundational to a resilient security culture. When individuals understand the implications of their actions and see the value in adopting secure behaviours, they are more likely to commit to a security-first approach.

The benefits of a security-conscious culture extend beyond merely mitigating risks. Organisations with strong security cultures often experience better overall performance, as the efficiencies and disciplines that come with good security practices can positively impact other business areas.

Looking to the future, organisations with an integrated security-conscious culture are better positioned to thrive amid evolving security threats. This approach not only defends against current threats but also prepares an organisation to adapt to new challenges, embodying true resilience rapidly.

In summary, the journey towards enhanced security is both a technological and cultural endeavour. A cultural shift towards security consciousness is crucial for organisations aiming to stay ahead of the curve in a landscape marked by increasing and dynamic threats. By embedding security into the fabric of an organisation's culture, businesses can transform their employees from the weakest link in the security chain into their greatest asset.

Building a security-conscious culture is undoubtedly challenging. It requires commitment, leadership, and a willingness to invest as much in people as in technology. However, the rewards - resilience against threats, empowered employees, and a proactive security posture - far outweigh the efforts. In the face of an uncertain and risky future, a strong security culture is not just beneficial; it is essential for survival and success.

Chapter **2**

The Threat Landscape

In the last chapter, we discussed the evolving security landscape, highlighting the necessity for a cultural shift to enhance security measures. This chapter invites you to deepen your comprehension of modern security leaders' challenges.

At the heart of crafting a security-conscious organisation lies the imperative to recognise and dissect the nature of threats encircling our digital and physical environments. This chapter elucidates the spectrum of security threats - from cyber to physical and the intricate combined cyber-physical threats increasingly prevalent in our interconnected world.

Appreciating how swiftly emerging technologies introduce new vulnerabilities while automation and artificial intelligence reshape the security landscape with their potential and risks is imperative. Equally, understanding the human element, namely the behavioural insights and psychological factors underpinning security risks, is crucial in fortifying our defences.

As we journey through this chapter, let's equip ourselves with the knowledge to identify these threats, comprehend their potentially devastating impact, and lay the groundwork for a resilient security posture that anticipates and actively mitigates these evolving risks.

Modern Security Threats: An Overview

In this digital epoch, the landscape of security threats has morphed beyond recognition, requiring security leaders to be perpetually on their toes. Modern security threats are extensive, ranging from sophisticated cyber-attacks designed to breach data integrity to physical threats that jeopardise our tangible assets. However, the advent of combined cyber-physical threats marks a particularly daunting evolution, where adversaries exploit interconnected systems to launch multi-faceted assaults on organisations.

Understanding the nature of these threats is fundamental in this context. It's about recognising the 'how' and the 'why' behind the attacks. This insight empowers you to anticipate vulnerabilities, strengthen your defences, and foster a culture of resilience.

Remember, in the face of modern security threats, knowledge is not just power - it's protection. By staying informed and adapting to the ever-changing threat landscape, you and your organisation can bolster your security measures, safeguarding your digital and physical realms against today's sophisticated threats.

Cyber threats evolve with alarming sophistication, making them one of the most significant concerns for business leaders worldwide. The landscape is ever-changing, so staying ahead requires a deep understanding of what these threats entail and how they operate. Cyber threats range from malware attacks, which can cripple entire systems, to social engineering tactics that manipulate individuals into divulging confidential information. These threats don't discriminate, targeting organisations of all sizes across various industries.

In addressing cyber threats, it's crucial to recognise that technology alone cannot be a panacea. While essential, the human element plays a pivotal role in cybersecurity. Often considered the weakest link in security chains, employees can be transformed into an organisation's most robust defence with the right training and mindset. This underscores the necessity for a security-conscious culture that prioritises continuous education on the significance of cybersecurity measures and practices.

The rise of remote work has further complicated the cyber threat landscape. As organisations shift to digital platforms, vulnerabilities increase, providing cybercriminals new opportunities to exploit. Phishing attacks, for instance, have become more sophisticated, leveraging the current global climate to create highly convincing scams. This calls for a vigilant and informed workforce that can promptly recognise and respond to such threats.

Data breaches are another critical concern, with consequences that can devastate an organisation's reputation and financial well-being. Protection against such breaches requires robust technological safeguards, strict data management policies, and a culture that values and protects information as a vital asset.

Ransomware attacks, in which attackers lock organisations out of their systems and demand a ransom for access restoration, highlight the need for robust backup strategies and incident response plans. Such plans should be in place, regularly updated, and practised to ensure they are effective under stress. The key is responding to attacks and anticipating and preventing them where possible.

Emerging technologies also introduce new vulnerabilities, necessitating continual learning and adaptation. For example, adopting Internet of Things (IoT) devices increases the potential attack surface for cybercriminals. Here, security by design becomes critical, integrating security measures from the development stage of products and systems.

The competitive advantage gained by organisations that foster a security-conscious culture cannot be overstated. This culture protects against immediate threats and builds resilience against future challenges. This resilience becomes a cornerstone of trust between the organisation and its clients, stakeholders, and employees.

Leadership plays a critical role in developing a security-conscious culture. By leading by example and ensuring that cybersecurity is a strategic priority, leaders can inspire their teams to adopt and maintain high-security standards. Investment in training and awareness programs and creating clear policies and practices that guide behaviour in day-to-day operations are essential.

As we look towards the future, the importance of a proactive approach to cybersecurity becomes even more apparent. The landscape will continue to evolve, and with it, so will the types of threats organisations face. Staying informed and agile, ready to adapt strategies and practices, is the only way to stay ahead. This requires constant vigilance and a commitment to embedding security into the fabric of organisational culture.

In summary, cyber threats pose a formidable challenge that can be mitigated with the right mix of technology, education, and cultural adaptation.

Physical threats in security pertain not merely to the tangible and immediate dangers that can compromise an organisation's safety but also to the overarching need for a strategic framework that acknowledges these risks as critical components of security management. As we delve deeper into understanding these threats, it becomes apparent that they span a wide range, from natural disasters to malicious acts of terror, each requiring a bespoke approach to mitigation and resilience building.

The first line of defence against physical threats is often the physical security measures that an organisation implements. This entails everything from access control systems to surveillance cameras to intrusion detection systems. However, leaders must recognise the symbiotic relationship between these physical security measures and the broader organisational culture of security awareness. Creating a culture where every employee understands their role in maintaining security is not just beneficial; it's essential for ensuring these physical defences are effective.

Moreover, the evolving nature of physical threats necessitates an equally dynamic approach to security strategy. The traditional model of 'fortressing' - building more barriers and isolating assets - is no longer sufficient in an age where threats can be as diverse as drone overflights or cyber-physical attacks. Thus, we must foster an environment of continuous learning and adaptation, where security practices are regularly reviewed and updated in response to emerging physical threats.

At the heart of effectively managing physical threats lies the principle of resilience. It's not solely about preventing every possible threat but also about how quickly and efficiently an organisation can recover when a physical threat does materialise. Therefore, resilience planning involves risk assessment and mitigation, business continuity planning, and recovery strategies that span the entire organisation. Leaders play a crucial role in championing these resilience efforts, ensuring they are woven into the fabric of the organisation's culture.

Combined cyber-physical threats refer to incidents where a cyberattack directly impacts physical security or vice versa. A quintessential example involves a company's digital infrastructure breach, leading to the physical manipulation or sabotage of critical hardware. These scenarios are not simply hypothetical; they are real-world challenges organisations face today. As such, an integrated approach to security, encompassing both cyber and physical aspects, is essential.

To combat these threats effectively, leaders must recognise the interconnected nature of their systems. Infrastructure such as power grids, water treatment facilities, and industrial control systems are often managed through networked devices. An intrusion into this network can allow attackers to cause physical damage, disrupt essential services, or even endanger lives. Therefore, mitigating such threats requires a holistic security strategy that does not treat cyber and physical security as discrete entities.

In conclusion, the threat landscape for modern organisations includes dangers that span both the cyber and physical domains. Addressing these combined threats requires a concerted effort and a unified approach to security practices. By recognising the interdependencies of their systems, adopting a proactive security posture, and fostering a resilient organisational culture, leaders can better protect against the multifaceted risks of today's interconnected world. This holistic perspective is not only a strategic imperative but a fundamental pillar for any entity aiming to thrive amidst the complexities of the 21st century.

The Impact of Technology on Security

As we navigate the tides of digital transformation, it's paramount to acknowledge the dual-edged nature of technology's impact on security.

On one hand, innovative technologies offer unprecedented opportunities to fortify our defences against a myriad of threats. For instance, advancements in encryption, threat detection algorithms, and blockchain technologies have profoundly reshaped the landscape of cyber security, providing businesses with robust tools to safeguard their information integrity.

On the other hand, this relentless tide of technological innovation invariably brings new vulnerabilities. Cybercriminals employ increasingly sophisticated methods, leveraging the same technologies to orchestrate greater complexity and scale attacks. Consequently, the task for IT, business, and security leaders is to embrace these technological advances and to do so with a keen awareness of the potential risks involved.

Cultivating a security-conscious organisation in today's digital age means understanding how emerging technologies can fortify and compromise organisational security. We must ensure that as we ride the wave of technological advancement, we maintain sight of the shore of security resilience.

Emerging Technologies and New Vulnerabilities

As we delve deeper into emerging technologies, leaders must comprehend the new vulnerabilities these technologies introduce. This understanding is crucial; it's foundational to building a security-conscious organisation. Rapid technological evolution brings many complex security challenges, thus necessitating a proactive and informed approach to cybersecurity.

The advent of the Internet of Things (IoT) has exponentially increased the number of connected devices, each representing a potential entry point for cyber threats. These devices often lack robust security features, making them vulnerable to attacks. Organisations are responsible for securing these devices, necessitating constant vigilance and regular updates to security protocols.

Artificial Intelligence (AI) and Machine Learning (ML) have transformed several operational aspects, allowing for predictive analytics and more personalised customer experiences. However, these technologies also give rise to unique vulnerabilities. AI systems can be manipulated; for example, adversarial attacks can deceive AI models into making incorrect decisions. Businesses must be vigilant and ensure their AI systems are designed with security, including implementing mechanisms to detect and mitigate such manipulation.

Blockchain technology has been heralded for securing transactions and reducing fraud through its distributed ledger system. Yet, it's not without its vulnerabilities. The immutability of blockchain can become a liability if incorrect data is entered, and smart contracts, while powerful, can contain flaws that hackers can exploit. Understanding these nuances is key to leveraging blockchain securely.

Quantum computing, a technology still in its infancy, promises to revolutionise computing by making processing power exponentially faster. However, it also poses a significant threat to current encryption methods. Organisations must stay ahead of the curve by researching quantum-resistant encryption methods to protect sensitive information in a future where quantum computing is commonplace.

Cloud computing has become a staple for storing data and running applications, offering flexibility and scalability. Yet, the shared responsibility model of cloud services means organisations must be acutely aware of their role in securing data. Misconfigurations and inadequate access controls in cloud environments are common vulnerabilities that can lead to data breaches.

5G technology promises faster connectivity and the ability to support many IoT devices. However, it also introduces new security challenges, including increased attack surfaces and the potential for more sophisticated cyber-attacks. Organisations must adapt their security strategies to address these risks, including implementing more robust encryption methods and continuously monitoring network activity.

Supply chain attacks have gained prominence. In these attacks, attackers target less secure elements in the supply chain to compromise the final product. Emerging technologies exacerbate this vulnerability, as organisations rely on third-party components and software. A holistic approach to security, including vetting third-party vendors and components, is essential to mitigate this risk.

Deepfakes, generated by AI, present a new form of threat where audio and video can be manipulated to create convincingly fake content. This can lead to misinformation, reputational damage, and even security breaches through manipulated identity verification processes. Awareness and the development of detection tools are critical in combating deepfake-related threats.

As we incorporate more autonomous systems and robots into operational processes, the potential for sabotage or accidental harm due to security lapses increases. Ensuring these systems have built-in security measures and can operate safely, even in the event of a compromise, is paramount.

Biometric security systems are becoming more prevalent, offering a seemingly secure authentication method. Nevertheless, these systems can be vulnerable to spoofing, and once biometric data is compromised, it cannot be changed like a password. Protecting biometric data with strong encryption and secure storage practices is vital.

Edge computing, processing data closer to where it's generated rather than in a centralised data centre, reduces latency and disperses the security perimeter, making it more challenging to manage. Robust security protocols must be implemented locally, and data encryption must be a priority to protect against interceptions and breaches.

Finally, the rise of smart cities and connected infrastructure introduces various cybersecurity challenges. The interconnectivity of services and systems increases the potential impact of a cyber-attack, highlighting the need for comprehensive security strategies encompassing the entire ecosystem.

In summary, while emerging technologies offer tremendous benefits, they also introduce new vulnerabilities that must be addressed. The call to action is clear: stay informed, anticipate future vulnerabilities, and implement proactive security measures. Embracing these challenges as opportunities to innovate and strengthen security postures will help better protect your organisation.

Automation, AI, and security implications

In the whirlwind of technological advancements, automation and artificial intelligence (AI) have emerged as pivotal forces driving change across industries. Their integration within organisational frameworks is not just transformative; it's revolutionising the way businesses operate, introducing efficiencies and capabilities that were once deemed futuristic. However, this digital transformation also brings forth complex security challenges that must be meticulously navigated to safeguard the assets and integrity of businesses.

At the heart of this technological evolution, automation employs algorithms and machines to perform tasks that traditionally required human intervention, streamlining operations and reducing the scope for error. Parallelly, AI - with its capability to learn, adapt, and make decisions - ushers in an era of intelligent automation. This synergy between automation and AI can significantly enhance organisational performance and expand the attack surface for potential cyber threats.

One of the key security implications of deploying automation and AI lies in the inherent vulnerabilities of these technologies. AI systems, for instance, are only as good as the data they are trained on. If this data is biased or manipulated, it could lead to flawed decisions, making AI-driven systems susceptible to unique forms of attack, such as data poisoning. Additionally, the complexity of these systems can make it difficult for security teams to fully understand or anticipate all potential vulnerabilities, thereby complicating the task of safeguarding them.

Moreover, using automation and AI in security operations is a double-edged sword. On the one hand, it enables the analysis of vast quantities of data at unprecedented speeds, identifying potential threats with a level of efficiency that human operators cannot match. On the other hand, reliance on these technologies can create a false sense of security, leading organisations to overlook the importance of human intuition and oversight in detecting nuanced or evolving threats.

While advantageous for growing businesses, the scalability of these technologies also poses a security risk. As organisations deploy these technologies across various facets of their operations, they must also scale their security measures accordingly. This requires a dynamic approach to security, where strategies are continuously updated to address emerging threats and vulnerabilities.

Furthermore, integrating these into business operations can significantly change the workforce dynamic. As certain tasks become automated, the role of human employees evolves, necessitating a shift in the skills required for effective security management. This transition challenges organisations to ensure their teams are adequately trained and equipped to manage the security demands of an increasingly automated and AI-driven work environment.

Data privacy concerns also surge with the adoption of these technologies. The vast amounts of data collected and processed by these technologies are valuable to businesses and cybercriminals. Ensuring the privacy and security of this data is paramount, requiring robust mechanisms to prevent unauthorised access and breaches.

Regulatory compliance becomes another critical consideration. As governments and regulatory bodies introduce new laws to address these technologies' privacy and ethical implications, businesses must stay abreast of these developments. Non-compliance poses legal risks and can damage an organisation's reputation and stakeholder trust.

Leaders must foster a culture of security awareness where the implications of automation and AI on security are recognised and addressed at every level of the organisation. This involves investing in the right technologies and frameworks and ensuring employees are educated and empowered to contribute to a secure digital environment.

Collaboration between IT and security teams is essential. These teams must work in tandem to assess the security implications of new technologies, implement appropriate safeguards, and respond swiftly and effectively to any incidents. Such collaboration fosters a holistic approach to security, leveraging the strengths of automation/AI and human oversight.

Continuous monitoring and assessment of security protocols are crucial in an environment enriched with AI and automation. As attackers evolve their tactics to exploit new vulnerabilities, security strategies must be regularly reviewed and updated. This dynamic approach to security ensures that organisations can adapt to the continuously changing threat landscape, maintaining the integrity and resilience of their operations.

Investing in cybersecurity R&D is another strategic imperative for mitigating risk. By dedicating resources to research and development, organisations can stay ahead of emerging threats, developing innovative solutions that protect against current threats and are adaptable to future challenges.

Moreover, engaging with external security experts and industry forums can provide valuable insights into managing security implications. These interactions can offer fresh perspectives, benchmarking opportunities, and access to shared resources that enhance an organisation's security posture.

Automation and AI are transforming the business world, offering unparalleled opportunities for growth and innovation. However, the security implications of these technologies necessitate a comprehensive and dynamic approach. By recognising the challenges and actively engaging in strategic planning, leadership, and continuous learning, organisations can harness the benefits of automation and AI while ensuring their assets remain protected in a digital-first world.

Behavioural Insights into Security Risks

In unveiling the complex tapestry that security risks present, one can't overlook the quintessential role of human behaviour. At the heart of many security breaches lies a technological failure *and* a human one. Psychology and cybersecurity intersect in this realm, shedding light on how cognitive biases, decision-making processes, and socio-psychological factors significantly elevate an organisation's vulnerability. Understanding these behavioural dimensions underpins the development of more resilient and adaptive security strategies.

By recognising that employees can be the weakest link of the first line of defence, businesses are equipped to foster a culture where security-conscious behaviour becomes second nature. This approach enhances an organisation's ability to ward off threats and nurtures an environment where security and business objectives are aligned.

Emphasising the human element in security risk management encourages a shift from merely reactive measures to proactive, behavioural-change-driven strategies that safeguard both digital and physical realms.

Understanding human factors in organisational security isn't just an optional extra; it's a vital component of a robust defence against today's ever-evolving threats. CEOs, IT heads, and security leaders must grasp that the weakest link in any security chain is often not the technology but the people who use it. This insight forms the backbone of creating a security-conscious culture within the organisation.

Humans, by nature, are creatures of habit and comfort. This behavioural pattern extends into the digital realm, where convenience often trumps security considerations. Common practices such as using simple passwords, reusing them across multiple platforms, or clicking links without due diligence contribute significantly to security vulnerabilities. Furthermore, the emotional aspects of human behaviour, such as trust and fear, can be exploited by cybercriminals through tactics like phishing or social engineering.

Understanding these human factors demands a shift from a purely technological focus to a more holistic view of security. It involves delving into behavioural science to understand why people make certain decisions that may compromise security and how their behaviour can be nudged towards more secure practices. This approach recognises that awareness and training are about dispensing knowledge and changing behaviours and mindsets.

For organisations, the starting point is to assess the current state of security awareness and practices among their employees. This assessment can highlight areas of vulnerability that stem from human factors. For instance, if a significant portion of the workforce is prone to using weak passwords, the focus can be on educating them about the importance of strong, unique passwords and providing tools like password managers to facilitate this behaviour.

The principle of least privilege is another crucial concept in mitigating the risks associated with human factors. It entails giving employees access only to the information and resources necessary for their job roles, thereby limiting the potential damage from insider threats or accidental breaches.

Incentivising secure behaviour can lead to positive outcomes. When employees understand that their actions contribute to the company's overall security posture and are recognised for their proactive security behaviours, it fosters a security culture. This can be achieved through recognition programs, rewards, or even gamification strategies.

Security training programs need to be engaging, relevant, and continuous. One-off training sessions or monotonous lectures will not suffice. Instead, incorporating interactive elements, real-life scenarios, and tests can help reinforce learning. Regular updates are also necessary to keep pace with evolving threats and security at the top of everyone's mind.

Leadership is pivotal in reinforcing the importance of understanding human factors in security. Leaders must exemplify secure behaviours themselves and be active sponsors of security initiatives. Their commitment can drive home the message that security is a collective responsibility, not just the domain of the IT or security department.

Emotional intelligence in leadership is also paramount when dealing with human factors. Leaders need to understand and manage their own emotions and those of their employees, especially in the context of security. They should foster an environment where employees feel comfortable reporting security incidents or potential threats without fear of retribution. Such an approach can significantly enhance the effectiveness of an organisation's security posture.

Feedback mechanisms should be instituted to learn from security incidents and near misses. These mechanisms can provide valuable insights into how human factors contribute to security breaches and what preventive measures can be taken. An open culture that encourages sharing and learning from mistakes can transform those incidents into powerful lessons for the entire organisation.

The psychological concept of 'social proof' can be utilised to bolster security practices. Employees who see their peers engaging in secure behaviour are more likely to follow suit. Highlighting stories of positive security behaviours within the organisation can leverage this social proof and encourage a more security-conscious culture.

Understanding the diverse cultural backgrounds present within a global organisation is also critical. Cultural differences can influence attitudes towards security, risk, and compliance. Therefore, security training and initiatives must be tailored to respect and address these cultural nuances so that the workforce can effectively absorb them.

The integration of technology can support the human side of security. Tools that simplify secure behaviour, such as two-factor authentication apps, email filters that flag phishing attempts, and security dashboards, can reduce the cognitive load on employees and make it easier for them to practice secure behaviour consistently.

Finally, measuring the impact of efforts to address human factors in security is essential. This could involve tracking metrics such as the number of reported phishing attempts, adherence to password policies, or the outcomes of simulated phishing exercises. These measurements can inform the organisation about the effectiveness of its initiatives and highlight areas for further improvement.

The role of psychology in security vulnerabilities

As we delve into the intricate dynamics of security vulnerabilities, it's essential to acknowledge the profound impact of psychology. The intersection between human behaviour and security isn't merely coincidental; it's foundational. Understanding the psychological underpinnings of vulnerability exploitation enables leaders to fortify their organisations more effectively against cyber threats.

Security isn't solely a technical challenge; it's a human one. Simple human errors or manipulation can undo the most sophisticated security systems. Psychological principles, such as trust, fear, and reward, play pivotal roles in how security breaches occur and propagate. Phishing attacks, for example, exploit trust and curiosity, luring individuals into disclosing confidential information.

Moreover, the concept of social proof, where individuals tend to follow the actions of others, can lead to security lapses. If employees notice their peers bypassing security protocols for convenience, they're more likely to emulate these actions, believing them acceptable. This herd mentality can significantly undermine security efforts.

Anchoring bias, where individuals rely too heavily on the first piece of information they receive, can also jeopardise security. An initial assurance of a system's security, despite subsequent advisories of vulnerabilities, may prevent individuals from acknowledging the real risks, leading to complacency.

The principle of authority is another psychological factor influencing security. Employees might unquestioningly follow instructions from what appears to be a legitimate authority figure, such as a manager or CEO, without verifying the requests' legitimacy. Authority phishing attacks exploit this vulnerability.

The fear of missing out (FOMO) can additionally drive individuals to take unwise security risks. Cyber attackers often create a sense of urgency or offer too-good-to-miss opportunities that prompt quick, ill-considered actions, such as clicking on a malicious link.

Security strategies must incorporate psychological insights into their design and implementation to counter these vulnerabilities. This includes understanding common cognitive biases and designing systems and protocols resilient to technical attacks and psychological manipulation.

Creating a security culture within an organisation involves more than just setting policies; it requires changing behaviours. This behavioural change is deeply rooted in psychological principles. By recognising and addressing the underlying psychological factors, leaders can foster a more security-conscious mindset among their staff.

Engaging and motivating employees to follow security practices are challenges that can be addressed through psychological approaches. Techniques from behavioural science, such as nudging and positive reinforcement, can more effectively encourage the adoption of secure habits than traditional methods, such as fear-based communication or strict policy enforcement.

Moreover, the effort to understand the psychology behind security vulnerabilities extends to designing security training programs. Training should inform and transform perceptions, making security a personal value rather than a mere obligation. Training programs can achieve a more profound, more lasting impact by appealing to intrinsic motivations and demonstrating the relevance of security to personal and organisational well-being.

Leadership plays a crucial role in embedding a security-conscious culture. Through their actions and communications, leaders can model security behaviours that reflect an understanding of psychological drivers and barriers. By being transparent about security challenges and how they are addressed, leaders can build trust and promote a more open and proactive security stance within their teams.

Understanding the psychology behind security vulnerabilities also aids in anticipating potential threats and crafting pre-emptive measures. By analysing behavioural trends and psychological triggers, security teams can predict how attackers might exploit human weaknesses and develop defences accordingly.

Mitigating security risks involves an ongoing education, reinforcement, and adaptation cycle. As the psychological landscape evolves - influenced by societal changes, technological advancements, and emerging threats - so must our approaches to security awareness and behaviour change.

Finally, a psychologically informed security strategy recognises the diversity of human behaviour and tailors its approaches to accommodate a wide range of attitudes and behaviours. This personalised approach enhances the effectiveness of security measures and fosters a more inclusive and adaptable security culture.

How Bad Can It Get When It Goes Wrong?

When cybersecurity fails due to cultural or behavioural shortcomings, the consequences can be financially and operationally catastrophic. Here are some examples that illustrate the severe impacts of such failures:

Target Data Breach (2013)[1]

Target's failure to act on early warnings from its security systems exposed 40 million credit and debit card numbers. The cultural failure to prioritise and act on cybersecurity alerts caused significant financial losses and damaged customer trust. This case demonstrates how ignoring security protocols can amplify the impact of a breach.

Equifax Data Breach (2017)[2]

The Equifax breach exposed the personal information of 147 million people. Although the failure to update a critical software vulnerability was pinned on a single employee, the incident highlighted a broader cultural issue within the organisation. The breach resulted in costly legal

---

[1] https://www.darkreading.com/cyberattacks-data-breaches/target-ignored-data-breach-alarms

[2] https://www.darkreading.com/perimeter/equifax-breach-underscores-need-for-accountability-simpler-architectures

settlements and severe reputational damage, showcasing how a lack of accountability and poor communication can lead to devastating outcomes.

DISH Network Ransomware Attack (2023)[3]

DISH Network's ransomware attack disrupted operations, and reports suggest that a ransom might have been paid to prevent the release of stolen data. The incident underscores the high stakes when an organisation's cybersecurity culture does not effectively address ransomware threats. It also highlights the operational paralysis that can occur without robust defences.

Microsoft Data Exposure (2023)[4]

Microsoft AI researchers inadvertently exposed 38 terabytes of sensitive data due to a misconfiguration when publishing files on GitHub. This incident is a prime example of how even the most technologically advanced companies can fall victim to cultural oversights, such as inadequate checks and balances on data handling practices.

---

[3] https://www.bleepingcomputer.com/news/security/dish-slapped-with-multiple-lawsuits-after-ransomware-cyber-attack/

[4] https://thehackernews.com/2023/09/microsoft-ai-researchers-accidentally.html

Tesla Insider Data Theft (2023)[5]

Two former Tesla employees leaked confidential data, exposing the personal information of nearly 76,000 employees. This incident highlights the risk of insider threats and the need for a security culture with stringent access controls and monitoring. The financial and reputational damage from such incidents can be profound, as seen in Tesla's case.

These examples demonstrate how deeply cultural and behavioural failures impact an organisation's cybersecurity posture. When employees are not adequately trained, security alerts are ignored, or access controls are lax, the door is left wide open for cybercriminals. The resulting breaches can lead to massive financial losses, operational disruption, and long-term reputational damage.

For organisations looking to avoid similar fates, these cases are a stark reminder of the importance of fostering a proactive and vigilant cybersecurity culture.

In conclusion, the role of psychology in security vulnerabilities is profound and pervasive. By embracing a psychologically informed perspective, leaders can craft more resilient, adaptive, and human-

---

[5] https://www.infosecurity-magazine.com/news/tesla-insiders-responsible-for/

centric security strategies. By understanding the human factors contributing to security risks, organisations can become more resilient to the types of cyber threats seen across the media today.

Chapter 3

Foundations of a Security Culture

Establishing a robust security culture is paramount in the journey to resilience against cyber threats. This chapter delves into the bedrock principles and strategies that are pivotal in nurturing a security-centric mindset across an organisation. The essence of a resilient security culture is not just about implementing the right tools and technologies; it's about shaping the way individuals perceive, value, and engage with security in their daily professional undertakings. The collective commitment to security, from the boardroom to the break room, underpins the success of any security strategy, turning reactive measures into proactive resilience.

Central to fostering this culture is the principle of continuous education, aimed at equipping every member of the organisation with not only the knowledge but also the critical thinking skills necessary to recognise and mitigate potential security threats. However, knowledge alone isn't enough. The challenge lies in effectively engaging and motivating employees to take personal responsibility for security. This entails moving beyond traditional didactic training methods to more interactive, participatory approaches that underscore the relevance of security in the personal and professional spheres. Such strategies amplify the message that security isn't solely the domain of the IT department but a shared organisational value.

Leaders must embody the security principles they wish to instil within their teams, advocating for best practices and exemplars of the security culture in action. This requires a shift in leadership training to include a strong emphasis on security awareness and cultivating skills necessary to inspire and sustain a security-conscious environment. Encouragingly, the seeds sown by committed leadership can yield a perceptive and proactive security posture across the organisation, thereby fortifying its defences against the ever-evolving landscape of cyber threats.

Principles of a Resilient Security Culture

In forging ahead from understanding the multifaceted nature of security threats and recognising the impact of cultural dimensions on security, it becomes imperative for leaders to embed resilient principles into the organisational ethos. This section delineates the foundational principles of a resilient security culture, serving as a cornerstone for cultivating a security-conscious organisation.

First and foremost, a resilient security culture is predicated on inclusivity. Security is not the sole preserve of the security and IT departments; it's a shared responsibility that permeates every level of the organisation. Inclusivity ensures that every individual understands their role in the organisation's security posture, regardless of their role. This collective responsibility fosters a sense of belonging and ownership among staff, which is crucial for active participation and vigilance in a resilient security culture.

The second principle revolves around continuous education and awareness. The digital landscape is ever-evolving, with unprecedented new threats emerging. A resilient security culture invests in ongoing education initiatives that keep everyone abreast of the latest threats and best practices for prevention and response. Tailoring training to diverse roles within the organisation ensures relevance and effectiveness, making security awareness a part of the organisational DNA.

Adaptability is another cornerstone principle. Just as cyber threats evolve, so must an organisation's security strategies. A resilient security culture is dynamic and capable of adapting to changes in the threat landscape and within the organisation itself. This involves staying current with technological advancements and being prepared to re-evaluate and adjust policies and strategies in response to new information or changing circumstances.

Transparency within the organisation is essential for fostering trust and accountability. This principle encourages open dialogue about security policies, incidents, and improvements. By demystifying security processes and decisions, organisations can empower their staff, build trust, and promote a more engaged and proactive stance toward security matters.

Risk awareness and management form the bedrock of a resilient security culture. Understanding that not all risks can be eliminated but managed and mitigated is vital. This principle entails identifying, assessing, and prioritising risks and implementing strategies to minimise their impact. It's about making informed decisions that balance risk with opportunity rather than pursuing security at all costs.

The principle of proactivity versus reactivity is critical. A resilient security culture anticipates threats and acts in advance to prevent them rather than merely responding after the fact. This proactivity is supported by threat intelligence, scenario planning, and regular security assessments to identify potential vulnerabilities and threats before they can be exploited.

Technology integration with cultural initiatives underscores the symbiotic relationship between technological solutions and the human element in cybersecurity. Leveraging technology to enhance security measures, automate repetitive tasks, and provide real-time threat analysis complements cultural efforts by freeing human resources to focus on strategic initiatives and complex problem-solving.

Commitment from leadership is indispensable. Leaders must not only endorse but actively participate in and model the behaviours and attitudes they wish to see throughout the organisation. Their involvement demonstrates the importance placed on security, reinforcing its value and encouraging alignment across all levels of the organisation.

Finally, resilience in security culture is built on a foundation of feedback and iteration. A culture that learns from its successes and failures continuously refining its approaches based on feedback and new insights, is better positioned to evolve and strengthen over time. This principle ensures that security practices remain effective and relevant, fostering a culture of continuous improvement.

Inculcating these principles within an organisation takes time. It requires concerted effort, strategic planning, and unwavering commitment at all levels. However, its dividends in enhanced security posture, reduced risk, and overall organisational resilience are invaluable.

As we proceed, it's crucial to remember that implementing these principles will vary from one organisation to another, influenced by factors such as size, industry, and cultural specifics. Nevertheless, the underlying tenets remain universally applicable and offer a blueprint for building a resilient security culture that can withstand the challenges of today's dynamic threat landscape.

Embedding these principles into your organisation's fabric sets the stage for the strategic and behavioural shifts necessary for a robust security culture. It lays the groundwork for preventing security breaches and enabling your organisation to thrive in an era where digital threats are an ever-present reality.

Strategies for Mindset Change

In the quest to fortify an organisation against cyber threats, the transformation of the collective mindset stands as a formidable pillar within the foundations of a security culture. Achieving a paradigm shift from seeing security as a technical issue to recognising it as a core aspect of organisational life requires strategic manoeuvring. To embark on this journey, it is essential to anchor change in the understanding that every employee, regardless of their role, is a custodian of the organisation's security. One effective strategy is the implementation of comprehensive educational initiatives. Cultivating an environment where knowledge sharing is continuous and engaging encourages a natural curiosity about security matters. Moreover, simplifying complex security concepts to ensure they are accessible to all plays a crucial role in demystifying security and embedding it into the fabric of everyday work life.

Another critical strategy is encouraging employees to adopt and advocate for secure practices. This can be achieved by aligning security behaviours with intrinsic motivations and the organisation's values. Recognising and rewarding security-conscious behaviours reinforces their importance and taps into the powerful human drive for acknowledgement and appreciation. Furthermore, creating narratives around the impact of secure practices on protecting personal and organisational assets can galvanise employees, fostering a culture where security is viewed as a shared responsibility. Engaging storytelling techniques and showcasing real-world examples of security breaches and their impacts can serve as potent tools in highlighting the tangible benefits of a proactive security stance.

Leaders must embody the security principles they wish to instil within their teams, demonstrating commitment through actions and words. Training leaders to communicate the importance of security in a manner that resonates with different audiences ensures the message is received and acted upon. Additionally, empowering leaders to act as change agents by fostering open dialogue about security challenges and successes fosters an environment of trust and collaboration. When leaders champion security, it sets a powerful precedent, reinforcing its significance as a cornerstone of the organisational ethos. Through educational initiatives, engaging and motivating employees, and exemplary leadership, the bedrock for a resilient security culture can be laid, leading to a more safeguarded future.

Educational Initiatives

Education is the cornerstone of cultivating a security-conscious organisation. It's about more than imparting knowledge; it's about shaping mindsets and fostering a culture where security is woven into daily operations. In this section, we delve into the various educational initiatives that can guide leaders to fortify their organisations against cyber threats.

First, it's essential to acknowledge the diversity in learning styles within any organisation. A one-size-fits-all approach to education won't cut it. Developing a multifaceted educational program that incorporates various learning methods, including workshops, e-learning modules, interactive sessions, and real-life simulations, is crucial. These initiatives ensure that employees understand their role in safeguarding the organisation's assets and are also engaged and motivated to act on this knowledge.

Interactive workshops are a particularly effective tool in the security education arsenal. They offer a hands-on learning experience that can be tailored to the organisation's specific needs. By simulating real-life scenarios, employees can better comprehend the complexities of security threats and the importance of their response. It's one thing to read about a phishing attack; it's another to experience it in a controlled, educational setting where the immediate consequences of one's actions are evident.

E-learning modules provide the flexibility crucial in today's fast-paced work environments. They allow employees to learn at their own pace and on their own time, which can dramatically increase the uptake of security best practices. However, it is important to ensure these modules are engaging and regularly updated to reflect the latest security threats and defences.

Another aspect of educational initiatives that must be considered is the role of leadership in promoting a culture of security. Leaders should be seen as enforcers of security protocols and active proponents and role models. Tailored training for leaders can empower them to lead by example, demonstrating the importance of security in their day-to-day decisions and actions.

Establishing a continuum of learning is beneficial for further embedding security into the organisational culture. This means going beyond the initial training and incorporating security education into the organisation's daily life. Regular updates, tips, and reminders about security can be disseminated through various channels such as newsletters, intranet posts, or team meetings. This keeps security front of mind and reinforces the message that security is everyone's responsibility.

Recognition and rewards can also be crucial in reinforcing positive security behaviours. Employees who exemplify strong security practices or actively contribute to the organisation's security culture can be acknowledged through awards or other incentives. This motivates individuals and sets a benchmark for others to aspire to.

Peer-to-peer learning is another powerful method to enhance security education. When employees share their knowledge and experiences with their colleagues, it can lead to a deeper understanding and more personal investment in the subject matter. Creating forums for this type of exchange, such as security champions networks or discussion groups, can be highly beneficial.

It's also imperative to measure the effectiveness of educational initiatives. With proper metrics and benchmarks, it's easier to gauge the impact of these programs on the organisation's security posture. Surveys, quizzes, and incident response drills can provide valuable feedback on progress and identify improvement areas.

Adopting a proactive approach to security education is also key. This means not waiting for a security breach to occur before acting but rather continuously seeking opportunities to enhance security awareness and skills within the organisation. Organisations can stay one step ahead of cybercriminals by anticipating future threats and educating employees on safeguarding against them.

The integration of technological solutions with educational initiatives cannot be ignored. Leveraging the latest technology to deliver training programmes can make learning more accessible and engaging. For example, virtual reality simulations of cyber-attacks can offer an immersive learning experience that is hard to match with traditional methods.

Customisation of educational content is crucial. Given the varied roles within an organisation, the security risks and responsibilities can differ significantly. Tailoring the educational content to address the specific threats and practices relevant to different departments ensures that the training is appropriate and effective.

Finally, fostering a culture of continuous learning is essential. Security threats are constantly evolving, and so must our knowledge and defences against them. Encouraging a mindset where learning and adaptation are valued over complacency can help build a more resilient organisation.

Inspirational success stories from within the organisation or other companies can be powerful motivators. Sharing these stories during training sessions or through company communications can highlight the real-world impact of effective security and inspire employees to emulate such success.

Engaging and Motivating Employees

Engaging and motivating employees are pivotal pillars in shaping a resilient organisational culture to cyber threats. For leaders, fostering an environment where every employee feels part of the security solution rather than seeing security protocols as hindrances is imperative. This section will explore strategies to achieve this, offering guidance tailored to enhance your organisation's defence against the ever-evolving landscape of security risks.

Communication and education are at the heart of engaging employees in cybersecurity. However, these should not be approached as one-off tasks but as ongoing efforts that adapt to technological changes and shifts in the organisational culture. Informing staff about the potential risks and their role in the organisation's security is just the starting point. Creating platforms for ongoing dialogue about security, where employees can voice concerns and contribute ideas, is equally vital. This approach demystifies cybersecurity, making it a collective responsibility.

Recognition is crucial in motivating employees to adopt and maintain security best practices. When employees demonstrate a proactive stance on cybersecurity, acknowledging their efforts can reinforce positive organisational behaviour. This recognition can come in different forms, from formal reward systems to informal peer recognition in meetings or internal communications. By celebrating these victories, you signal to your team that their contributions make a significant difference in maintaining the organisation's security posture.

Implementing gamification techniques can further enhance engagement and motivation. You transform learning and compliance from tedious tasks into engaging activities by introducing elements such as leaderboards, badges, or rewards for completing security-related challenges or training. This method makes learning more enjoyable and fosters a healthy competitive environment that can effectively drive positive behavioural changes.

Empowering employees is another critical strategy. When individuals feel they have the power to effect change and their actions are instrumental in the organisation's security, they are more likely to take ownership of their roles. Empowerment can take many forms, such as giving employees autonomy to make security-related decisions or involving them in developing security policies. This inclusion improves the policies by incorporating diverse perspectives and boosts employees' commitment to adhering to them.

Training and continuous learning opportunities are essential for keeping employees engaged and motivated in the long term. Security landscapes and the knowledge and skills of those tasked with safeguarding the organisation evolve. Offering regular training sessions, workshops, and seminars that cover the latest trends and threats in cybersecurity can keep the workforce not just informed but also interested.

Creating a culture of psychological safety is paramount for an engaged workforce. Employees should feel comfortable reporting security concerns or breaches without fear of reprimand. Establishing clear channels for such reports and a supportive response strategy encourages a proactive approach to identifying and mitigating risks.

Leadership involvement cannot be overstated in its importance. When leaders exemplify a strong commitment to cybersecurity, it sets a powerful example for the rest of the organisation. Leaders should be accessible and actively participate in security training and initiatives, demonstrating that security is a priority at all levels of the organisation.

Feedback mechanisms are practical tools for gauging employee engagement and the effectiveness of motivational strategies. Regular surveys, suggestion boxes, or feedback sessions can provide valuable insights into the workforce's perception of security initiatives and identify areas for improvement. This feedback not only aids in refining strategies but also makes employees feel valued and heard, further enhancing their motivation.

Another aspect to consider is customising engagement tactics to fit the diverse needs of your workforce. Different departments or roles may face unique security challenges, and acknowledging these differences through tailored engagement and training can significantly increase their effectiveness.

Highlighting the broader impact of cybersecurity efforts can also be a strong motivational factor. Helping employees understand how their actions contribute to the security of the organisation and protecting clients, society, and national security can instil a sense of purpose and pride in their roles.

In summary, engaging and motivating employees in cybersecurity is more than a one-size-fits-all endeavour. It requires a multifaceted approach that considers your workforce's diverse motivations and learning preferences. By implementing a combination of communication, recognition, empowerment, and continuous learning, you can foster a security-conscious, resilient culture that is responsive to the changing threat landscape.

Ultimately, the goal is to transform cybersecurity from being perceived as a set of restrictive rules into a shared value and mission. Fostering this shift through sustained effort and leadership is possible and essential for your organisation's long-term security and success.

The journey towards creating a security-conscious organisation doesn't end here. As outlined in the subsequent chapters, our exploration of behavioural science, technological integration, and the role of security champions will further enrich your strategy, providing the tools and insights necessary to navigate the complex terrain of cybersecurity in our modern world.

In essence, the task ahead is challenging yet deeply rewarding. You are laying the cornerstone for a resilient security culture by effectively engaging and motivating your employees. Remember, a well-informed, motivated, and proactive workforce is your best defence against cyber threats, transforming potential vulnerabilities into strengths.

As we progress, let's remember that cybersecurity is not just about protecting information or technology but safeguarding trust, integrity, and the continuity of our operations. The strategies and principles outlined in this and subsequent chapters will guide you towards achieving these objectives, ensuring your organisation remains vigilant and adaptable in the face of ever-changing threats.

Leadership in Security Culture

At the crux of fostering a robust security culture within any organisation is the pivotal role played by its leaders. Dynamic leadership is not merely about enforcing policies or ushering in new protocols; it's essentially about embodying the change one wishes to see. Business, IT, and security leaders are tasked with a significant and continual challenge: to inspire, influence, and inculcate a mindset that prioritises security at every turn. The cornerstone of this endeavour lies in understanding that leadership's commitment to and visible engagement with security initiatives sends a potent message throughout the organisation. It sets the tone for how security is perceived and acted upon at all levels.

Moreover, transforming an organisation's security culture demands that leaders are well-versed in the nuances of contemporary security threats and equipped with the knowledge and skills to guide their teams through the cultural shift needed. This entails a bespoke approach to training leaders for heightened security awareness. Leaders can foster a more resilient organisational fabric by enhancing their capability to identify, communicate, and mitigate risks. Encouraging open dialogue, leading by example, and rewarding proactive security behaviours are instrumental strategies. It's about building a culture where security becomes a shared responsibility, woven into the very fabric of daily operations rather than seen as a peripheral or solely IT-related issue.

Crucially, leadership in security culture champions integrating security into strategic decision-making processes. It involves a clear-eyed assessment of not only the technical but also the human factors influencing security. Through embedding security considerations into business objectives, performance metrics, and the organisation's value system, leaders can steer their teams towards a more security-conscious mindset. This holistic approach ensures that the commitment to security transcends individual departments and becomes a unifying goal, creating a truly resilient and security-savvy organisation. Ultimately, the strength of a security culture hinges upon the quality of its leadership – leaders who are not just enforcers but passionate advocates of security as a core organisational pillar.

The role of leadership in cultural change

In creating a security-conscious organisation, leadership isn't simply a role or a set of responsibilities; it's the bedrock upon which the security culture is built and sustained. As we navigate the complexities of instilling a robust security culture, the pivotal role of leadership in driving cultural change becomes evident. Leaders are not just enforcers of policies but visionaries who inspire, motivate, and steer their organisations toward a shared vision of resilience against cyber threats.

Leadership in cultural change begins with a demonstration of commitment. This commitment must be visible and unequivocal. Leaders must walk the talk by embedding security practices into their daily routines, making security a regular discussion topic, and leading by example. Such actions send a powerful message throughout the organisation: security is not optional; it's integral to how we operate.

However, leadership in fostering a security-conscious culture extends beyond individual conduct. It encompasses the creation of a strategic framework wherein security is seamlessly integrated into all aspects of the business. This means prioritising security initiatives, allocating appropriate resources, and ensuring security considerations are front and centre in decision-making processes.

Effective leaders understand the dynamics of change management. They recognise that cultural transformation entails alterations in procedures and, more importantly, shifts in values, attitudes, and perceptions. It's about cultivating a mindset wherein every organisation member perceives themselves as a vital link in the security chain.

Team empowerment is another critical aspect of leadership in cultural change. Leaders must empower their teams by providing them with the tools, knowledge, and authority to act on security issues. This involves investing in training and development programs, fostering an environment where questions and concerns about security are encouraged, and rewarding rapid response to security incidents.

Communication plays a crucial role in the effectiveness of leadership in cultural change. Clarity, consistency, and transparency in communication help demystify security and underscore its significance. Leaders should communicate the 'why' behind security policies and practices, making the rationale clear and compelling.

Building trust is fundamental. Trust is earned when leaders demonstrate accountability for security at the highest levels. This includes being open about security failures when they occur, learning from them, and taking decisive actions to prevent recurrence. Such openness fosters a culture of trust and learning rather than blame, encouraging more proactive disclosure and discussion of security concerns.

Leaders must champion innovation in driving cultural change. This means being open to new ideas, technologies and approaches to security. It involves creating a culture where experimentation is valued, and failure is seen as a step towards learning and improvement.

The inclusivity of leadership in cultural change can't be overstated. A security-conscious culture is where everyone feels included, valued, and heard. Leaders must ensure that security initiatives are inclusive, considering the organisation's diverse roles, responsibilities, and perspectives. This diversity of thought is critical in identifying potential security gaps and fostering innovative solutions.

Leadership also means building partnerships beyond the organisation. In today's interconnected world, a security-conscious culture extends to how an organisation interacts with its partners, suppliers, and customers. Leaders must champion initiatives that promote security consciousness across this extended ecosystem.

Monitoring and measuring the impact of cultural initiatives is another crucial role of leadership. Leaders should establish and review metrics that assess the effectiveness of security practices and culture. This not only helps identify areas for improvement but also celebrates successes, thereby reinforcing the value of the security culture.

Adaptability is a key leadership quality in the context of cultural change. The threat landscape and the organisation's security culture are constantly evolving. Leaders must be quick to identify shifts in the threat environment and agile in adapting policies, practices, and culture in response.

Finally, leadership in cultural change is about sustaining momentum. It's about continuously reinforcing the importance of security, celebrating wins, learning from setbacks, and reminding everyone that security is a shared responsibility. Leaders must cultivate resilience within their teams, ensuring the security culture is robust enough to withstand challenges and evolve.

As we explore the strategies and practices that can facilitate this transformation, we must remember that the tone is set from the top. The success of any cultural change initiative, especially in the security domain, hinges on the active participation, support, and leadership of those at the helm. Let this be a call to action for all leaders: to lead the charge in fostering a culture that views security not as a hurdle but as a cornerstone of success and sustainability in the digital age.

Training leaders for security awareness

As we've explored the essence of building a resilient security culture, it's imperative that we now focus on those at the helm - our leaders.

Leadership in any organisation isn't just about steering the ship; it's about recognising and navigating the icebergs of cyber threats that might lurk beneath seemingly calm waters. Training leaders for security awareness is not just an option but a necessity in today's digitally interconnected world.

Leaders are pivotal in setting the tone for an organisation's security posture. Their commitment to security awareness is reflected significantly across all levels of the organisation. However, cultivating this awareness isn't merely about attending workshops or seminars but embedding a proactive security mindset into every decision and action. Leaders must exemplify the cybersecurity behaviours they wish to see throughout their organisation.

To effectively train leaders for security awareness, organisations must first ensure that these programmes are tailored to align with their specific business context and risks. Generic training content doesn't just miss the mark; it also risks disengaging your leadership. This tailored approach helps highlight the real and relevant threats an organisation faces, making the training more impactful.

Interactive and engaging training methods have proven more effective than traditional lecture-based sessions. Simulated cyber-attack exercises, for example, place leaders in the hot seat, compelling them to make critical decisions in real time. This experiential learning approach fosters a deeper understanding of the implications of those decisions and actions in the context of security.

Leaders must also be trained to recognise the often-subtle indicators of security risks. This includes understanding attackers' psychological tactics, such as phishing scams, which often exploit human emotions like fear or urgency. Equipping leaders with the skills to spot these tactics can prevent potential breaches before they occur.

Training should also include guidance on compliance and the legal implications of data breaches. This knowledge ensures leaders protect their organisation's assets, reputation, and legal standing.

The role of empathy in leadership training cannot be understated. Leaders should be encouraged to understand and appreciate their teams' challenges in maintaining security protocols. This empathy can lead to more supportive environments where employees feel valued and understood, strengthening the organisation's security culture.

One of the most crucial aspects of training is continuity and refreshment. Cyber threats constantly evolve, and so must our understanding and strategies to counteract them. Regularly updating training content and conducting refresher sessions can keep leaders sharp and prepared for new types of attacks.

Feedback mechanisms should also be incorporated into the training programmes, allowing leaders to share their insights and experiences. This feedback can be invaluable in refining the training content and making it more relevant and effective.

Accountability is another critical component. Leaders should be encouraged to set security-related objectives for themselves and their teams and integrate these goals into performance evaluation processes. This emphasises the importance of security and fosters a culture of accountability at all levels.

Moreover, training should also extend beyond the cyber domain to include physical security awareness. In an era where physical and cyber threats are increasingly intertwined, leaders should be equipped to understand and mitigate risks across both fronts.

Diversity of thought and approach in training methodologies is also beneficial. By incorporating perspectives from different departments, geographies, and industries, they can gain a broader understanding of security challenges and innovative ways to address them.

In addition to in-house training, leaders should be encouraged to participate in external educational opportunities. Industry conferences, webinars, and certifications can provide valuable insights into cybersecurity trends and best practices.

Finally, it's vital to foster an environment where learning from failures is seen as an opportunity for growth. Leaders should be taught that setbacks can be valuable learning experiences in cybersecurity, contributing to a more robust security posture in the future.

Chapter 4

Introducing Behavioural Science

In the quest to fortify organisations against cyber threats, it's imperative to harness the power of behavioural science. This discipline offers invaluable insights into why individuals act the way they do, especially in the context of security. To change security behaviours effectively, one must appreciate that human behaviour isn't solely based on logic or understanding; emotions, habits, and the environment play a significant role. Applying behavioural science in security initiatives can identify the leverage points for encouraging a security-conscious culture. This chapter introduces behavioural models and theories before delving into the strategies for applying principles to design interventions that inform and inspire lasting behavioural changes. Through understanding the psychological underpinnings of actions, leaders can craft messages and systems that resonate on a deeper level, making security practices more intuitive and embedded within daily routines.

However, creating interventions that stick requires more than just insight; it necessitates a thoughtful design that considers the end-to-end experience of those it's meant to influence. This is where the concept of *designing for stickiness* comes in. It's about creating security practices and messages that are memorable, engaging, and capable of nudging behaviour in the long term. Incorporating technology as an enabler is crucial in this endeavour. You must look beyond technology as merely a tool for enforcing security measures, viewing it to enhance understanding, provide consistent reminders, and facilitate easier adoption of security behaviours. Best practices for technology deployment include integrating behavioural cues into existing workflows and using data analytics to personalise security messages, making them more relevant and impactful to everyone.

Lastly, the success of any behavioural intervention must be quantifiable. Measuring the cultural impact on security is essential for demonstrating value and guiding continuous improvement. This involves establishing clear metrics and benchmarks for success, such as reductions in phishing susceptibility or increases in secure password adoption. However, it's not just about tracking adherence to specific practices; it's also about gauging shifts in attitudes and perceptions towards security within the organisation. Continuous improvement in security practices is achieved through a cycle of measuring, learning, and adapting - ensuring that interventions remain effective and responsive to the evolving security landscape and organisational culture. This chapter will guide leaders through the intricacies of integrating behavioural science into their security strategy, designing interventions that resonate with employees, and leveraging technology to solidify and measure the cultural shift towards a security-conscious organisation.

Introduction to Behavioural Models and Theories

Behavioural science studies human behaviour and decision-making, encompassing various disciplines such as psychology, sociology, and economics. By applying behavioural science principles, organisations can better understand the factors that influence employees' attitudes and behaviours towards cyber security, thereby enabling the design of more effective interventions to promote secure practices. This section will explore commonly used theories, methodologies, and frameworks within behavioural science and demonstrate how they can be applied to cyber security culture and behavioural change. Additionally, we will discuss more modern research and its implications for building a robust cybersecurity culture.

The Theory of Planned Behaviour

One of the most widely used behavioural science theories is the Theory of Planned Behaviour (TPB), developed by Ajzen (1991)[6]. The TPB posits that an individual's behaviour is influenced by three factors: attitudes towards the behaviour, subjective norms, and perceived behavioural control. In the context of cyber security, this theory suggests that employees' intentions to engage in secure practices are shaped by their beliefs about the importance of these practices, the expectations of others (e.g., peers, supervisors), and their confidence in their ability to perform these practices.

For example, if employees perceive that following cyber security protocols is essential for the organisation's success (attitudes), believe that their colleagues and superiors expect them to adhere to these protocols (subjective norms), and feel capable of following these

---

[6] Ajzen, I. (1991). The theory of planned behaviour. *Organizational Behavior and Human Decision Processes*, 50(2), 179-211.

protocols without undue difficulty (perceived behavioural control), they are more likely to engage in secure behaviour.

In applying the TPB to cyber security, organisations can focus on interventions that target these three factors. Educational campaigns can enhance positive attitudes towards cyber security, while social influence strategies, such as creating a culture of accountability and recognition, can strengthen subjective norms. Additionally, providing adequate resources and training can improve employees' perceived behavioural control, increasing their likelihood of complying with security measures.

Social Cognitive Theory

Bandura's (1986) Social Cognitive Theory (SCT) emphasises the role of observational learning, self-efficacy, and reinforcement in behaviour change[7]. In cyber security, SCT can be applied by encouraging positive role modelling and creating environments that reinforce secure behaviour. Employees who observe their peers and leaders consistently practising good cyber hygiene are likelier to adopt these behaviours.

Self-efficacy, or an individual's belief in their ability to perform a specific behaviour, is also crucial in SCT. Enhancing employees' confidence in

---

[7] Bandura, A. (1986). *Social foundations of thought and action: A social cognitive theory*. Prentice-Hall.

their ability to protect themselves and the organisation from cyber threats through targeted training and support can lead to sustained behavioural change. As Bandura states, *"People's beliefs in their efficacy influence the choices they make, their aspirations, how much effort they put forth in given endeavours, how long they persevere in the face of obstacles, and their resilience to adversity"* (p. 26).

The COM-B Model and the Behaviour Change Wheel

The COM-B model, developed by Michie, van Stralen, and West (2011), provides a comprehensive framework for understanding behaviour change by focusing on three key components: Capability, Opportunity, and Motivation. According to this model, behaviour (B) is a result of an individual's physical and psychological capability (C), the opportunities (O) afforded by their environment, and their motivation (M) to perform the behaviour.

The COM-B model can be utilised in cyber security to design interventions that address these three components. For example, capability can be enhanced through training programmes that improve employees' knowledge and skills in recognising and responding to cyber threats. Opportunities can be created by fostering an organisational environment that supports secure practices, such as providing easy access to security resources and reducing barriers to secure behaviour. Motivation can be strengthened through incentives, feedback, and communication strategies highlighting cyber security's importance and alignment with organisational goals.

The Behaviour Change Wheel (BCW), also developed by Michie et al. (2011)[8], builds on the COM-B model by providing a systematic approach to designing behaviour change interventions. The BCW includes nine intervention functions, such as education, persuasion, and environmental restructuring, which can be applied to influence behaviour. Using the BCW, organisations can develop tailored interventions that address specific behavioural challenges in their cyber security culture.

Nudge Theory

Thaler and Sunstein's (2008) Nudge Theory[9] has gained prominence recently as a method for subtly influencing behaviour without restricting choices. Nudge Theory suggests that small, well-designed interventions (nudges) can guide individuals towards making better decisions by leveraging cognitive biases and heuristics.

---

[8] Michie, S., van Stralen, M. M., & West, R. (2011). The behaviour change wheel: A new method for characterising and designing behaviour change interventions. *Implementation Science*, 6(1), 42.

[9] Thaler, R. H., & Sunstein, C. R. (2008). *Nudge: Improving decisions about health, wealth, and happiness*. Yale University Press.

In cyber security, nudges can encourage secure behaviour by making it easier or more appealing. For example, default settings can be configured to maximise security, such as enabling multi-factor authentication by default. Additionally, timely reminders or prompts, such as pop-up messages encouraging password updates, can nudge employees towards more secure practices. As Thaler and Sunstein (2008) explain, "A nudge is any aspect of the choice architecture that predictably alters people's behaviour without forbidding any options or significantly changing their economic incentives" (p. 6).

Modern Research and Emerging Trends in Behavioural Science

Although behavioural science and psychology are well-established fields with a long history of research, they continue to advance and evolve. In parallel, cyber security researchers are increasingly exploring how these disciplines can be applied to foster behavioural changes within the context of cyber security. Contemporary research and trends in this area focus on aspects such as behavioural insights, behavioural segmentation, the impact of emotions on behaviour, the influence of organisational identity, and the use of adaptive and personalised security interventions.

Behavioural insights, often called "behavioural economics," combine psychology and economics to understand how people make decisions. In cyber security, behavioural insights can be applied to identify and address cognitive biases that lead to risky behaviour. For example, the optimism bias, where individuals underestimate the likelihood of adverse events happening to them, can result in employees neglecting security measures.

Organisations can conduct behavioural experiments, such as A/B testing, to test different interventions and determine the most effective in promoting secure behaviour. By systematically testing and refining interventions, organisations can develop evidence-based strategies more likely to succeed in changing behaviour.

Behavioural Segmentation

Recognising that different employees may have different attitudes, knowledge levels, and motivations regarding cyber security, behavioural segmentation allows organisations to tailor interventions to specific groups. Organisations can design more targeted and effective interventions by segmenting the workforce based on factors such as risk perception, compliance history, and technological proficiency.

For instance, more tech-savvy employees may benefit from advanced training on emerging threats, while those less familiar with technology may need more foundational education on basic security practices. By addressing different segments' specific needs and characteristics, organisations can ensure that their interventions are more relevant and impactful.

The Role of Emotions in Cyber Security Behaviour

Recent research has highlighted the role of emotions in cybersecurity decision-making. Fear, for example, can be a powerful motivator for behaviour change but can also lead to counterproductive outcomes, such as avoidance or denial. A study by Pfleeger and Caputo (2012)[10] found that while fear-based messaging can initially grab attention, it may only lead to long-term behaviour change if accompanied by actionable steps and support.

Therefore, organisations should balance the use of fear with positive reinforcement and practical guidance. By creating a supportive environment that acknowledges the emotional aspects of cyber security, organisations can help employees feel more confident and empowered to engage in secure behaviour.

---

[10] Pfleeger, S. L., & Caputo, D. D. (2012). Leveraging behavioural science to mitigate cyber security risk. *Computers & Security*, 31(4), 597-611.

The Influence of Organisational Identity

Another emerging area of research focuses on the relationship between organisational identity and cyber security behaviour. Employees who strongly identify with their organisation are more likely to adopt behaviours that align with organisational values, including secure practices. As Ashforth and Mael (1989) note, "Organisational identification leads to internalisation of organisational values and norms" (p. 21)[11].

To leverage this, organisations can work to strengthen employees' identification with the organisation through initiatives that promote a sense of belonging and shared purpose. When employees see cyber security as part of their contribution to the organisation's success, they are more likely to prioritise it in their daily activities.

Adaptive and Personalised Security Interventions

Modern research increasingly emphasises the need for adaptive and personalised security interventions. Instead of one-size-fits-all approaches, organisations are exploring ways to tailor security measures

---

[11] Ashforth, B. E., & Mael, F. (1989). Social identity theory and the organisation. *Academy of Management Review*, 14(1), 20-39.

and messaging to individual employees based on their behaviour, preferences, and risk profiles.

For instance, personalised security dashboards that provide real-time feedback on an employee's security practices can encourage better decision-making. Additionally, adaptive training programmes that adjust content and difficulty based on an employee's progress can ensure that training remains relevant and challenging.

Applying Behavioural Science to Change Security Behaviours

Applying behavioural science is a pivotal strategy to fortify organisations against a myriad of cyber threats. This approach leverages a deep understanding of human behaviour to instigate and solidify positive security practices across an organisation. The journey requires insight, precision, and persistence, but the rewards for enhanced resilience are invaluable.

At the heart of behavioural science is the recognition that individuals are not always rational actors. People make decisions based on complex factors, including emotions, biases, and social influences. This reality often leads to less-than-optimal security behaviours. The challenge, then, is to navigate these human intricacies to promote behaviours that safeguard rather than endanger an organisation.

The first step in this transformative process is identifying the specific behaviours that need to change. This may include practices as simple as using strong, unique passwords or as complex as recognising and reporting phishing attempts. These behaviours must be clearly defined and communicated in a way that resonates with employees at all levels.

The next critical phase is understanding the barriers and motivators influencing these behaviours. Barriers can be anything from a lack of awareness about the risks to perceived inconvenience associated with securing behaviour. Conversely, motivators might include a desire to protect personal and organisational data or avoid a security breach's negative consequences.

With a firm grasp of the desired behaviours and the factors influencing them, the next step is to design interventions that leverage these insights. This might involve changing the organisation's environment to make the desired behaviour easy and natural. For instance, implementing password managers can alleviate the burden of remembering complex passwords, thus reducing a significant barrier to secure behaviour.

Another effective strategy is utilising social proof and norms to influence behaviour. Humans are inherently social creatures, and the perception of 'normal' behaviour within a group can have a powerful effect on individual actions. Highlighting stories of positive security behaviours and recognising individuals who exhibit them can encourage others to follow suit.

Feedback loops also play a crucial role in sustaining behavioural change. Regularly providing individuals with clear, constructive feedback on their security behaviours reinforces these actions' importance and helps embed them as habits. This feedback should be timely and specific, linking behaviours to outcomes whenever possible.

Importantly, behavioural interventions must be dynamic and adaptable. As threats evolve and organisations change, so must the strategies to promote secure behaviours. This requires ongoing assessment and refinement of interventions, underpinned by a commitment to continuous improvement.

Education and training are also indispensable tools in the behavioural science arsenal. Interactive and engaging training programmes can be particularly effective beyond mere information dissemination by simulating real-life scenarios. These experiences help cement knowledge and skills, making them more likely to be applied in practice.

Leadership engagement is essential for catalysing and sustaining behavioural change. Leaders must exemplify the desired behaviours, demonstrating a genuine commitment to security that inspires others to follow their lead. Moreover, leaders are pivotal in creating a culture where security behaviours are valued and rewarded.

It's vital to adopt a multidisciplinary approach to truly integrate behavioural science into security strategies. Collaboration with psychology, communications, and even design experts can enhance interventions' effectiveness. This cross-pollination of ideas and expertise enriches the strategies, making them more nuanced and powerful.

Technological solutions also support behavioural changes. However, it's important to view technology not as a panacea but as a tool that must be wielded wisely. The best technological interventions seamlessly complement and enhance the behavioural strategies rather than attempting to replace them.

Measuring the impact of behavioural interventions is critical to understanding their effectiveness. This can be challenging, given the often intangible nature of behavioural change. However, combining qualitative and quantitative methods can provide a broad picture of progress. Surveys, interviews, and observational studies can yield insights into changing attitudes and behaviours, while metrics such as the frequency of security incidents can offer more objective measures of impact.

Finally, it's crucial to remember that changing security behaviours through behavioural science is challenging. It requires patience, persistence, and a willingness to learn and adapt. But the potential rewards - a more secure organisation resilient to cyber threats-are well worth the effort.

Designing Interventions That Stick

In security, it's quintessential that interventions designed to change behaviour take hold immediately and remain effective over time. The challenge here lies not just in the initiation but in the sustainability of these interventions. For leaders looking to forge a security-conscious organisation, understanding how to design these interventions is key to resilience against cyber threats.

The science of behaviour tells us that for any intervention to stick, it must be memorable and meaningful. Humans are creatures of habit; thus, interventions must seamlessly integrate into daily routines, becoming as natural and indispensable as checking emails first thing in the morning.

Firstly, the messaging behind the intervention must resonate on a personal level. Employees must understand the 'what' and the 'why' behind the measures. When people comprehend the direct impact of their actions on the organisation's overall security, their motivation to comply increases significantly.

An effective strategy involves framing the interventions regarding gains rather than losses. The Psychology of behaviour change shows that individuals are more motivated by the prospect of a gain (e.g., contributing to the company's security posture) rather than avoiding a loss (e.g., preventing a potential cyber-attack). This positive framing can significantly impact the uptake and adherence to security practices.

Moreover, engaging and involving employees in designing and implementing security measures can foster a sense of ownership and commitment. When employees feel they have a stake in the security of their environment, they're more likely to adhere to the necessary protocols.

Feedback loops are crucial in reinforcing desired behaviours. Regular updates on how individual efforts make a difference can motivate continued compliance and tweak interventions as needed. Constructive feedback helps refine strategies and make necessary adjustments to ensure interventions remain relevant over time.

Incorporating elements of gamification can also enhance the stickiness of interventions. Leaderboards, rewards, and recognition for compliant behaviour can embed security practices into the corporate culture.

Gamification taps into natural human desires for competition and achievement, making compliance more engaging and less of a chore.

It's also important to recognise that one size doesn't fit all. Tailoring interventions to fit your organisation's and its employees' unique structure is fundamental. Different departments might face varying levels of risk or have different attitudes towards security, and interventions should be adapted accordingly.

When it comes to designing interventions, simplicity is the ultimate sophistication. Complex procedures are likely to be met with resistance or bypassed entirely. The easier and more intuitive the process, the higher the likelihood of adoption and perseverance.

Continuous education is pivotal in keeping security interventions at the forefront of mind. Regular training sessions, updates, and reminders about security protocols ensure that the information remains current and accessible.

Utilising technology as an enabler can significantly enhance the effectiveness of behavioural interventions. Automated systems that prompt users to update passwords, verify identities or encrypt emails can embed secure practices without relying wholly on human memory or compliance.

Anticipation of behavioural fatigue is crucial. Over time, even the most engaged employees can become desensitised to security alerts and protocols. Keeping interventions dynamic and adjusting strategies based on feedback and evolving threats can help maintain vigilance and interest.

Leadership plays a crucial role in the success of any intervention. Leaders must embody the security practices they wish to see, providing a visible template for behaviour within the organisation. Their commitment can inspire and motivate employees to follow suit.

Finally, measuring the impact of interventions is vital. Establishing clear metrics for success enables organisations to track progress, understand the effectiveness of different strategies, and identify areas for improvement. Regular assessments can ensure that interventions stick and evolve, keeping pace with internal and external changes.

In conclusion, designing interventions that stick requires a thoughtful blend of psychology, behavioural science, user-centred design, and continuous evaluation. For leaders, the goal is to create an ecosystem where secure behaviour is not just a mandate but a shared value, deeply embedded in the organisational culture.

Technology as an Enabler

In the dynamic interplay between behavioural science and security, technology emerges as a pivotal enabler, empowering organisations to craft a more resilient defence against cyber threats. Within the framework of developing a security-conscious culture, technology mustn't be perceived merely as a tool but as a partner in the behavioural evolution process.

By integrating cutting-edge technologies with cultural change initiatives, businesses can provide fertile ground for security behaviours to flourish naturally. This symbiotic relationship offers a two-fold advantage: it not only makes security practices more efficient and effective but also embeds these practices into the everyday actions of employees, making security a fundamental aspect of the organisational DNA.

As we harness technology to tailor security interventions that resonate on a personal level, we set the stage for a transformation that is both deep-rooted and widespread. Leveraging technologies such as automation, artificial intelligence, and machine learning can significantly amplify the impact of behavioural strategies, ensuring that security measures are adopted and sustained over time.

The goal is clear: by embedding technology into an organisation's cultural fabric, we can exponentially enhance its security posture, crafting an environment where each team member actively participates in the security narrative.

Integrating Technological Solutions with cultural initiatives is pivotal in moulding a security-conscious organisation. Synthesising technological advancements with an enterprise's ingrained cultural ethos strengthens its defence mechanisms and propels it towards resilience against cyber threats. This integration, however, demands a clear understanding and strategic alignment of technology's role within the organisation's cultural fabric.

The journey begins with acknowledging that technological solutions are not standalone fixes but tools that can enhance and be enhanced by the organisation's cultural strengths. For instance, adopting cutting-edge security software isn't merely about upgrading the IT infrastructure; it's about how this technology can be harmonised with the behavioural patterns, attitudes, and values of those interacting with it daily.

Leaders must champion technological adoption and embody and promote the cultural shifts necessary for these technologies to be effective. This means leaders must proactively educate themselves and their teams about the benefits and implications of new security technologies, fostering an environment where questions and discussions about these tools are encouraged.

Educational initiatives thus become a cornerstone of integrating technology with culture. Tailoring these initiatives to suit an organisation's diverse learning preferences can significantly impact their effectiveness. Interactive workshops, seminars, and e-learning modules that elucidate the importance of security measures and the role of technology in maintaining these measures can galvanise a uniform cultural shift towards better security practices.

Engaging employees at every level is also critical. It's not enough for the IT department to understand and back these technologies; every organisation member should grasp their role in upholding security through technology. Creating a sense of ownership and responsibility across the organisation can create a cultural staple where security becomes everyone's business.

Moreover, feedback mechanisms should be established to ensure that the integration of technology and culture is a continuous cycle of improvement. Employees should be encouraged to voice their experiences, challenges, and suggestions regarding using security technologies. This feedback can serve as invaluable data to refine and customise technological solutions to better fit the organisation's cultural dynamics.

Incorporating behavioural insights into deploying and adopting technological solutions can significantly enhance their effectiveness.

Understanding the psychological drivers behind security complacency or resistance to new technologies allows leaders to craft more empathetic and engaging strategies that align with cultural values and norms.

One must consider the global landscape of security practices too. With organisations increasingly operating globally, recognising and respecting cultural diversity in the approach to technology integration becomes paramount. What works in one cultural setting may not necessarily translate to another, necessitating a flexible and adaptable approach to integrating technology and cultural initiatives.

Furthermore, the role of Security Champions within this integration cannot be understated. Identifying and training key technologically savvy and culturally influential individuals can bridge gaps between IT and the wider organisation, facilitating smoother adoption of security technologies and practices.

Thus, best practices for technology deployment should not be rigid blueprints but flexible frameworks that can be adapted based on cultural insights and feedback. This involves prioritising user-friendly technologies that align with users' daily routines, thereby reducing friction and fostering a positive security culture.

Measuring the cultural impact on security post-technological integration is also essential. Establishing metrics and benchmarks for success enables organisations to track the effectiveness of integrating technology with cultural initiatives. This highlights areas of success and pinpoints areas needing further cultural or technological adjustment.

Continuous improvement in security practices through regular reviews and updates of technological tools and cultural strategies ensures the organisation remains resilient against evolving cyber threats. Emphasising a perpetual learning and adaptation culture instils confidence and competence in handling security challenges.

Anticipating future threats by staying abreast of technological advancements and shifts in cultural paradigms is essential for future-proofing security. The integration process is thus a dynamic journey of adaptation, learning, and growth, with technology and culture at its core.

In summary, integrating technological solutions with cultural initiatives is not a one-off task but a continuous endeavour that demands commitment, creativity, and collaboration. As leaders, the symbiotic enhancement of technology and culture under your stewardship can pave the way for a security-conscious organisation adept at navigating the complex cybersecurity landscape of today and tomorrow.

This alignment not only fortifies the organisation's defences but also nurtures a resilient, knowledgeable, and engaged workforce dedicated to safeguarding the integrity and security of its assets.

Best Practices for Technology Deployment

Integrating technological solutions with cultural initiatives requires focusing on deployment methodologies that align with our overarching goals. Technology deployment can be a potent enabler for enhancing our security posture when executed with precision and strategic foresight. Herein, we will explore some essential practices that can guide you through the maze of technology deployment, ensuring that their organisations survive and thrive in the face of cyber threats.

Conducting a comprehensive needs assessment is fundamental to understanding your organisation's security requirements. This step involves identifying the critical assets that need protection, the potential threats to these assets, and the vulnerabilities that could be exploited. A tailored approach to technology deployment begins with a deep understanding of what you protect and why.

Engagement with stakeholders across the organisation is another crucial practice. Security isn't solely the domain of the IT department; it's a shared responsibility that requires input and cooperation from every corner of the business. By involving stakeholders in discussions about technology deployment, you garner support and buy-in and ensure that the solutions implemented are practical and meet the organisation's diverse needs.

Both current and future security scenarios should guide the selection of technology. In an era where technology evolves quickly, opting for scalable and adaptable solutions can safeguard your organisation against emerging threats. It's not just about addressing today's challenges but also about being prepared for tomorrow's vulnerabilities.

Technology must be seamlessly integrated into existing systems and processes. Disruption can often lead to resistance, making it challenging to adopt new security measures. Leaders must ensure that technology solutions enhance, rather than complicate, the user experience. This not only aids in smooth implementation but also fosters a security-conscious culture within the organisation.

Training and awareness cannot be overstated. Technology alone cannot fortify your organisation's defences; a well-informed workforce must complement it. Regular training sessions, updates, and drills should be instituted to familiarise employees with security protocols and the proper use of technological tools. Empowered employees are your first line of defence.

Finally, continuous monitoring and improvement are essential. Deploying technology is not a one-off task but an ongoing process. Regular audits, threat assessments, and updates are necessary to ensure your security measures remain robust and responsive to the evolving cyber landscape.

Measuring Cultural Impact on Security

Assessing the cultural impact on security practices is a pivotal strategy to bolster an organisation's resilience against cyber threats. This scrutiny renders quantifiable metrics that leadership can leverage to gauge the effectiveness of implemented policies and serves as a barometer for the organisation's collective security consciousness.

Leaders can set achievable benchmarks targeting incremental improvements by establishing a baseline of current security behaviours within the enterprise's cultural milieu. Success in this realm is often manifested through enhanced employee engagement in security protocols, a demonstrable reduction in security incidents, and increased proactive security measures taken by staff.

The journey towards embedding a robust security culture is iterative, necessitating continuous assessment and refinements. This process, informed by behavioural science, underscores the imperative of adapting interventions to align with the evolving organisational culture, ensuring that security practices resonate with and are embraced by the workforce. Through this meticulous calibration of cultural influences and security protocols, organisations can cultivate a more secure environment poised to counter the multifaceted threats of an ever-changing digital landscape.

Metrics and Benchmarks for Success

Establishing clear metrics and benchmarks is pivotal to gauging the success of our endeavours to create a security-conscious organisation. We must grasp the significance of these metrics and understand how to apply them effectively to our daily operations. This section delves into measuring the cultural impact on security, offering a roadmap to evaluate, refine, and enhance our security practices.

It's often said that what gets measured gets managed. However, determining what to measure presents a unique set of challenges in fostering a security-conscious culture. The first step is setting clear, attainable benchmarks that align with our overarching goals. For instance, a decrease in the number of security incidents over a given period can directly indicate the effectiveness of our cultural shift towards heightened security awareness.

Equally important is measuring employee engagement in security training programs. Engagement levels can be quantified through various means, such as participation, completion, and post-training assessment scores. Such metrics highlight the reach and impact of our educational initiatives and inform the necessary adjustments to enhance learning outcomes.

Another critical metric is the response time to potential security threats. A reduction in this timeframe indicates an improved organisational capability to identify and mitigate risks swiftly. It reflects the technical readiness and the organisational agility cultivated through a pervasive security culture.

We must also consider the frequency of security updates and patches as a benchmark for success. Regular updates testify to an organisation's commitment to maintaining robust defence mechanisms against emerging threats. While seemingly technical, this metric is deeply rooted in the cultural aspect of prioritising security across all levels of the organisation.

User behaviour analytics provide profound insights into the efficacy of our cultural transformation. Metrics such as the number of users practising secure password management or the reduction in instances of clicking on phishing emails offer tangible evidence of behavioural change. This shift in day-to-day actions among our workforce is the most authentic testament to the embedding of security into our organisational culture.

Leadership engagement in security initiatives is a metric and a benchmark for success. Senior leaders' active participation not only sends a strong message about the importance of security but also helps embed this mindset throughout the organisational hierarchy. Metrics in this area could include the percentage of leaders who have completed advanced security training or the frequency of security communication from leadership to staff.

Furthermore, innovation in security practices should be continually measured. This could involve tracking the implementation of new security technologies or techniques and evaluating their impact on enhancing security postures. It reflects an organisation's adaptability and proactive stance towards evolving security challenges.

Customer trust and confidence are also crucial benchmarks. Surveys and feedback mechanisms can gauge how external stakeholders perceive the organisation's commitment to security. Improvements in these areas often correlate with a thriving cultural shift towards security mindfulness within an organisation.

Another aspect to consider is the success rate of internal phishing simulations. These exercises are invaluable in gauging employees' alertness and preparedness to identify and respond to cyber threats. A decline in these simulations' success rate indicates an increasingly security-aware workforce.

The integration of security practices into daily work routines represents a significant benchmark. This can be assessed through regular audits and by observing the extent to which security considerations are embedded in project planning, development, and operational processes. It highlights the translation of a security-conscious culture into practical, everyday actions.

To continuously improve our security culture, we must establish benchmarks for periodic review and assessment of our security landscape. This involves looking at the present metrics and setting future goals that align with emerging security trends and organisational growth.

Incentivising and recognising security-conscious behaviours can also serve as an effective metric. We foster an environment that values proactive security measures by celebrating successes and making examples of positive security actions. The number of recognitions or awards related to security practices can be a tangible measure of cultural adaptation.

The organisation's resilience in the face of cyber incidents provides critical feedback on the efficacy of our security culture. Analysing the outcomes of such incidents, including the speed of recovery and minimal impact, offers insights into the real-world effectiveness of our security culture. We must view these incidents as challenges and opportunities for learning and improvement.

The journey to embedding a profound security culture within an organisation is both complex and nuanced. Leaders can navigate this path more effectively by establishing comprehensive metrics and benchmarks for success. These measures provide the critical feedback needed to adapt, innovate, and continually enhance our security postures. Let's commit ourselves to this journey, with the understanding that success in cultivating a security-conscious organisation is not only about mitigating risks but also about fostering an environment where security and business objectives are seamlessly integrated.

Continuous improvement in security practices is an essential principle for businesses keen on fortifying their defences against a perpetually evolving landscape of cyber threats. In this pursuit, iterative refinement and reassessment of security measures are beneficial and necessary. The idea that security practices can be set in stone is a fallacy in a world where threat actors constantly innovate to bypass existing safeguards.

At the heart of continuous improvement lies the ability to recognise and adapt swiftly to new threats. As we have explored in previous chapters, the dynamics of cyber threats are influenced by a myriad of factors, including technological advancements, changes in attacker methodologies, and organisations' ever-expanding digital footprint. Thus, it becomes imperative for businesses to cultivate a culture where security practices are regularly reviewed, updated, and enhanced.

The process of continuous security improvement necessitates a structured approach. This begins with the establishment of clear metrics and benchmarks for success. These metrics serve as indicators of the effectiveness of current security measures and highlight areas requiring attention or adjustment. Additionally, they foster a culture of accountability within the organisation, ensuring everyone understands their role in maintaining and improving security.

Engaging and motivating employees play a crucial role in this process. Security isn't solely the domain of IT; it is a collective responsibility that spans the entire organisation. Educational initiatives designed to enhance employees' understanding of current threats and safe practices can significantly bolster an organisation's security posture. Regular training sessions, updates, and workshops ensure that employees remain vigilant and informed.

Organisations should also leverage technology as an enabler to facilitate continuous improvement. Integrating advanced security technologies can automate the detection and mitigation of threats, reducing dependence on manual intervention and allowing for a more dynamic response to emerging threats. However, it is essential to maintain a balance, ensuring that technological solutions are complemented by human insight and intervention.

Leadership plays a pivotal role in embedding a culture of continuous improvement within an organisation. Leaders must demonstrate a commitment to security, not only in word but also in deed. This involves allocating the necessary resources for security initiatives, supporting ongoing education and training efforts, and leading by example. When leadership prioritises security, it permeates the organisational culture, creating an environment where continuous improvement is valued and practised.

Applying behavioural science to change security behaviours is another aspect of continuous improvement. Understanding the psychological factors influencing behaviour can help design interventions that effectively enhance security practices. Organisations can engender a more security-conscious workforce by identifying the behavioural barriers to security compliance and addressing them through targeted strategies.

In addition to internal efforts, continuous improvement in security practices also benefits from external collaboration. Sharing knowledge and insights with other organisations and industry bodies can provide valuable perspectives on managing security risks. This collaborative approach aids in benchmarking an organisation's security practices against industry standards and gaining insights into effective strategies employed by others.

Another critical aspect of continuous improvement is the establishment of feedback loops. Encouraging feedback from employees, customers, and partners on the effectiveness of security measures can provide actionable insights for refinement. This feedback mechanism should be bolstered by regular security audits and assessments, which provide a comprehensive view of the organisation's security posture and areas for improvement.

Technology deployment best practices must also evolve as part of continuous improvement efforts. With the rapid pace of technological advancement, what was considered a best practice a year ago may now be obsolete. Regularly updating these best practices ensures that security measures keep pace with technological innovations, mitigating emerging vulnerabilities.

Measuring cultural impact on security is an integral component of continuous improvement. Understanding how cultural shifts within the organisation influence security practices is crucial. This understanding can guide the adjustment of strategies to ensure they are culturally aligned and more likely to be embraced by the workforce.

Continuous improvement in security practices must be scalable and adaptable. As organisations grow and evolve, so must their approach to security. This scalability ensures that security measures remain effective regardless of size, structure, or business activity changes.

Pursuing continuous improvement in security practices is a journey rather than a destination. It requires dedication, vigilance, and a proactive stance towards security management. In doing so, leaders can foster resilient organisations that are well-equipped to navigate the complexities of the modern security landscape.

As we move forward, it's essential to remember that the success of these efforts hinges on a collective commitment to security as a shared responsibility. Through collaboration, education, and a steadfast focus on continuous improvement, organisations can achieve a level of security that protects their assets and supports their growth and innovation.

Chapter 5

The Seven Dimensions of Security Culture

Security culture refers to the collective attitudes, behaviours, knowledge, and actions of an organisation's members concerning cybersecurity. It is the shared commitment of every employee - from the C-suite to the front lines - to protect the organisation's information and systems. Unlike purely technical measures, security culture cannot be achieved by simply implementing a policy or deploying new software. It requires a long-term, strategic effort to align people's behaviours with security best practices, ensuring they understand their role in maintaining security and are motivated to engage in secure behaviours.

Organisations with a strong security culture exhibit several key traits. Employees consistently follow security protocols, are aware of potential threats, report suspicious activity, and feel accountable for protecting the organisation's assets. Conversely, organisations with weak security cultures often face challenges such as non-compliance with policies, a lack of security awareness, and minimal engagement with security initiatives. In these environments, even the best technology may fail to prevent breaches if employees neglect their security responsibilities.

A thriving security culture can be likened to an immune system: it detects, responds to, and mitigates threats before they cause damage. Just as a healthy immune system requires nourishment and care, so does a security culture. It must be nurtured through training, leadership, communication, and continual reinforcement. A strong security culture reduces the likelihood of breaches, ensures compliance with regulatory requirements, and fosters a proactive approach to security, where employees are not just passive participants but active defenders of the organisation.

Understanding security culture is about recognising its importance and knowing how to measure and improve it. One way to achieve this is by breaking down security culture into measurable components or dimensions. This approach allows organisations to diagnose their strengths and weaknesses and take targeted actions to bolster their culture where needed.

In this chapter, we will explore the seven dimensions of security culture, as outlined in the research conducted by CLTRe[12], a KnowBe4 company. These dimensions provide a comprehensive framework for assessing security culture, including *behaviour*, *attitudes*, *cognition*, *communication*, *compliance*, *norms*, and *responsibilities*. By understanding these dimensions, organisations can assess their security culture and develop strategic initiatives to strengthen it, ensuring that employees are empowered and engaged in protecting the organisation from cyber threats.

The following sections will delve into these seven dimensions, explaining how they contribute to a robust security culture and offering practical insights into how organisations can improve in each area.

---

[12] CLTRé. (2020). *The 7 dimensions of security culture* [Research paper]. KnowBe4. https://www.knowbe4.com/hubfs/CLTRe-The7DimensionsSecurityCulture-ResearchPaper.pdf

Behaviour

Behaviour is one of the most critical dimensions of security culture because it directly reflects how individuals within an organisation act in response to security policies, threats, and procedures. It represents the visible actions employees take, day in and day out, that either strengthen or weaken the organisation's security posture. While attitudes and knowledge are important foundations, behaviour - the tangible, real-world actions - ultimately determines whether security policies are effective.

The Role of Secure Behaviour

In a strong security culture, secure behaviours are ingrained in employees' daily routines. These behaviours might include locking computer screens when stepping away from a workstation, adhering to password management policies, refraining from clicking on suspicious links, or promptly reporting phishing attempts and other suspicious activities to the IT or security teams. These seemingly small, routine actions are essential for reducing the risk of cyber threats and data breaches.

On the other hand, insecure behaviours - whether due to negligence, lack of awareness, or deliberate non-compliance - can severely compromise an organisation's security efforts. A single mistake, such as using a weak password or failing to recognise a phishing email, can open the door to cybercriminals and lead to costly breaches. As such, improving employee behaviour is often one of the first priorities for organisations seeking to bolster their security culture.

The Influence of Other Dimensions on Behaviour

While behaviour is the most visible and measurable aspect of security culture, it is influenced by other dimensions - particularly attitudes, cognition, and norms. For example, employees with a positive attitude towards security are likelier to engage in secure behaviours because they understand and value the importance of following security protocols. Likewise, if employees possess a high level of cognition or knowledge about security risks and practices, they are better equipped to make informed decisions and exhibit the right behaviours.

Norms also play a significant role in shaping behaviour. If the majority of employees in a department regularly follow secure practices, such as using multi-factor authentication or locking their devices, this sets an expectation that others will do the same. Behavioural science teaches us that people tend to follow the actions of their peers, which means that strong security norms can create a ripple effect, encouraging secure behaviour across the organisation.

However, the reverse is also true - if insecure behaviours are common, they can become normalised, undermining security efforts. For instance, if employees frequently leave their desks without locking their computers, or if password-sharing is a common practice, these behaviours can become accepted as "normal" within the organisation, increasing the likelihood of a security breach.

Measuring and Encouraging Secure Behaviour

To improve security behaviour within an organisation, it is important to first assess the current state of behaviour through various methods. Regular audits, security simulations (e.g., phishing tests), and employee surveys can provide valuable insights into how well employees adhere to security protocols and where gaps may exist. For example, an audit may reveal that while most employees follow proper password procedures, a significant number fail to report phishing emails, highlighting an area where behaviour needs improvement.

Once behaviours have been assessed, organisations can develop targeted interventions to encourage secure practices. These interventions might include:

Training and Awareness Campaigns: Regular, engaging training sessions can educate employees about the importance of secure behaviours and provide them with the knowledge they need to act securely. For example, training on identifying phishing emails or avoiding social engineering attacks can directly influence employees' actions.

Behavioural Nudges: Small changes in the environment or workflow can encourage better security behaviour. For instance, implementing automatic timeouts that lock computers after a period of inactivity ensures that even if an employee forgets to lock their screen, the system will protect itself. Similarly, email systems that flag external senders or potential phishing attempts can serve as reminders to employees to act cautiously.

Gamification: Many organisations have successfully used gamification to incentivise secure behaviour. By introducing competitions, rewards, or recognition for employees who consistently follow best practices, organisations can create a positive feedback loop where secure behaviour is rewarded and reinforced.

Leadership Modelling: Leadership plays a pivotal role in shaping behaviour. When senior executives and managers actively demonstrate secure behaviours, it sends a powerful message that security is a priority at all levels of the organisation. Leadership modelling helps to set the standard and expectations for the rest of the workforce.

Monitoring and Feedback: Continuous monitoring of employee behaviour is essential to ensure that improvements are being made and that secure behaviour is becoming the norm. This could involve regular phishing tests to measure how employees respond to simulated threats or monitoring compliance with security protocols through system logs.

Providing timely feedback to employees when they fail to follow secure practices also helps reinforce the importance of security.

Addressing Non-Compliance and Insecure Behaviour

Despite efforts to encourage secure behaviour, there will always be instances where employees fail to comply with security protocols, intentionally or unintentionally. Organisations must have clear processes in place to address non-compliance without fostering a culture of fear or blame.

For unintentional mistakes - such as an employee falling victim to a phishing attack due to a lack of awareness - it is essential to treat the incident as a learning opportunity. Immediate remediation and follow-up training can help the employee understand the error and take steps to avoid similar mistakes in the future. A supportive, educational approach is more likely to result in long-term behavioural change than punitive measures.

However, deliberate non-compliance or wilful negligence must be handled more seriously. Employees who repeatedly ignore security policies or take risks compromising the organisation's safety must be held accountable. This may involve escalating the issue to HR, implementing more stringent monitoring, or taking disciplinary action. At the same time, it is crucial to investigate whether these behaviours stem from deeper issues - such as overly complex or inconvenient security policies - that need to be addressed at an organisational level.

The Long-Term Benefits of Secure Behaviour

When secure behaviour becomes the norm across an organisation, the benefits are substantial. Not only does it significantly reduce the likelihood of breaches, but it also creates a culture of shared responsibility, where every employee sees themselves as part of the security team. This proactive approach is far more effective than relying solely on technical solutions to protect the organisation.

Moreover, consistent secure behaviour builds trust with clients, partners, and regulators, who are increasingly concerned with how organisations handle sensitive data. Demonstrating a strong security culture can be a competitive advantage, showcasing the organisation's commitment to safeguarding information and maintaining compliance with industry standards and regulations.

Behaviour is at the heart of a strong security culture. While other dimensions, such as attitudes, cognition, and communication, contribute to shaping behaviour, employees' day-to-day actions ultimately determine an organisation's security resilience. By fostering secure behaviour through training, communication, and leadership, organisations can build a security-conscious workforce that actively protects the organisation from cyber threats.

Attitudes

Attitudes represent employees' beliefs, feelings, and perceptions toward security within an organisation. They form the underlying mindset influencing how individuals approach security tasks and responsibilities. A positive attitude toward security is critical because it motivates employees to engage in secure practices and follow policies, even when doing so may seem inconvenient or security threats are not immediately apparent.

While behaviour reflects the actions employees take regarding security, attitudes drive those behaviours. A workforce that views security as a priority and understands its importance is far more likely to adopt secure habits and comply with protocols. On the other hand, if employees view security as a burden or unnecessary, they are less likely to internalise secure practices, increasing the organisation's vulnerability to cyber threats.

The Impact of Attitudes on Security Culture

Attitudes are a foundational aspect of security culture. Employees with a positive attitude towards security are more likely to follow best practices, stay vigilant against potential threats, and support organisational efforts to maintain a secure environment. A positive attitude can lead to proactive behaviours such as reporting phishing attempts, using strong passwords, and regularly updating software - all essential to protecting the organisation from cyber threats.

Conversely, negative attitudes towards security can lead to complacency or outright resistance. Employees who see security protocols as unnecessary or overly burdensome may choose to bypass them, such as reusing passwords, disabling security features, or ignoring security awareness training. These behaviours can expose an organisation to data breaches, malware, or social engineering attacks.

Attitudes towards security are shaped by various factors, including leadership, communication, personal experiences with security, and the organisational culture at large. Understanding these factors and addressing negative attitudes is key to creating a security culture where everyone is committed to protecting the organisation.

Factors Influencing Security Attitudes

Several factors contribute to how employees perceive and respond to security measures. By understanding these factors, organisations can take steps to foster positive attitudes and mitigate the conditions that lead to negative perceptions.

Leadership Influence - Leadership plays a central role in shaping employees' attitudes toward security. When executives and managers visibly prioritise security and consistently communicate its importance, it sets the tone for the rest of the organisation. Employees are more likely to take security seriously when they see their leaders demonstrating commitment, whether through compliance with security protocols, participating in awareness training, or encouraging open discussions about security concerns.

On the other hand, if leaders downplay the importance of security or fail to follow protocols themselves, it sends a message that security is not a priority. Employees may then adopt a similar attitude, seeing security as an afterthought or someone else's responsibility.

Perceived Relevance - Employees are more likely to adopt a positive attitude towards security if they believe that security practices are directly relevant to their roles and to the organisation's success. For instance, a finance team handling sensitive customer data may quickly grasp the importance of secure data handling. In contrast, a marketing team may see security as less relevant to their day-to-day work. If security measures are perceived as disconnected from employees' tasks, they may view them as a hindrance rather than a necessity.

Ensuring that security training and communications are tailored to the specific roles within the organisation helps to address this issue. By showing employees how security impacts their specific tasks - whether handling customer data, managing financial transactions, or protecting intellectual property - organisations can build a more widespread sense of responsibility and relevance.

Communication and Education - How security is communicated within an organisation also significantly influences attitudes. Regular, clear, and transparent communication about security risks, policies, and incidents helps keep security top-of-mind for employees. Additionally, providing context - explaining why certain security measures are in place - can help employees understand the reasoning behind security policies, reducing resistance.

Education and training are key components of this. When employees are well informed about the latest cyber threats and understand their role in defending against them, they are more likely to develop a positive, proactive attitude towards security. However, if security policies are communicated top-down and overly technically without considering the employee's perspective, this can foster confusion or frustration, leading to a negative attitude.

Experience with Security Incidents - Employees who have personally experienced or witnessed a security breach, phishing attack, or data loss incident may have a heightened awareness of the importance of security, leading to a more positive attitude. These experiences often serve as wake-up calls, making employees more vigilant and willing to follow security practices in the future.

Conversely, employees who have not experienced any direct consequences of poor security may become complacent. The absence of perceived threats can lead to the belief that security is not a pressing issue. In such cases, it is essential to continuously remind employees of the potential risks and the broader impact of cyber threats on the organisation, even if they have not personally been affected.

User Experience with Security Tools - The usability of security tools and processes significantly impacts employee attitudes. If security systems are cumbersome, slow, or interfere with employees' ability to complete their work efficiently, they are more likely to develop negative attitudes. For example, if password management systems are difficult to use or multi-factor authentication (MFA) slows down access to necessary systems, employees may become frustrated and less inclined to comply with security measures.

Ensuring security tools are user-friendly and integrate seamlessly with daily workflows can improve employees' attitudes toward security. By minimising friction and making security as convenient as possible, organisations can reduce frustration and foster a more positive outlook on security practices.

Shifting Negative Attitudes Towards Security

For organisations aiming to build a stronger security culture, addressing negative attitudes is just as important as promoting positive ones. Negative attitudes towards security can arise from several factors, such as a lack of awareness, frustration with security tools, or a perception that security is the responsibility of the IT department alone. Addressing these concerns requires a multifaceted approach.

Engagement and Involvement - One effective way to shift negative attitudes is to involve employees in the conversation about security. When employees feel that their concerns and suggestions are heard, they are more likely to engage positively with security initiatives. For example, organisations can set up focus groups or surveys to gather employee feedback on security tools and policies. This participatory approach helps employees feel a sense of ownership and reduces the perception that security is a one-size-fits-all mandate imposed from above.

Incentives and Recognition - Recognising and rewarding employees who demonstrate secure behaviour can positively influence organisational attitudes. This could take the form of small incentives - such as public recognition in company newsletters, security awards, or even tangible rewards for employees who consistently follow security best practices. Such recognition reinforces that security is valued and individual contributions matter.

Security Champions Programmes - Another effective strategy is implementing a Security Champions programme, where employees across various departments serve as security advocates. These champions can help promote positive attitudes toward security by acting as role models, answering questions, and demonstrating secure behaviours within their teams. Having champions in place can help demystify security for employees and break down barriers between the IT and security departments and the rest of the workforce.

Training and Awareness Campaigns - Continuous training and awareness campaigns are essential for shaping positive attitudes. These campaigns should go beyond simply teaching employees about cyber threats; they should also focus on changing perceptions of security. For example, training sessions can highlight the personal and professional benefits of following security practices, such as protecting one's own personal data and avoiding the potential consequences of a security breach.

Regular updates and refresher courses can also help keep security top-of-mind, ensuring that employees remain engaged and aware of the importance of security in their day-to-day work.

Simplifying Security Processes - When possible, simplifying security processes can go a long way in reducing frustration and improving attitudes. For example, offering single sign-on (SSO) solutions or integrating MFA in a way that doesn't interrupt workflows can help reduce friction. Streamlining security processes ensures that employees don't feel security is an obstacle to their productivity, which in turn encourages a more positive attitude toward following security policies.

Measuring Attitudes Towards Security

To assess how employees feel about security, organisations can use surveys, focus groups, or one-on-one interviews. These assessments can help identify areas where attitudes may be particularly strong or weak, providing insight into where interventions are needed.

Questions could include:

- *How important do you feel security is in your role?*
- *Do you find security policies easy to understand and follow?*

- *How confident are you in identifying and reporting security threats like phishing emails?*
- *Do you believe leadership in the organisation prioritises security?*

By regularly measuring attitudes and tracking changes over time, organisations can evaluate the effectiveness of their security culture initiatives and identify areas for improvement.

The Long-Term Impact of Positive Attitudes

Fostering positive attitudes toward security has long-term benefits for organisations. When employees are engaged with and motivated by security, they are more likely to follow best practices, comply with policies, and act as the first line of defence against cyber threats. This proactive mindset significantly enhances the organisation's security posture, reducing the likelihood of costly breaches or incidents.

Moreover, a workforce with positive attitudes towards security is more adaptable to changes in security policies, tools, or threats. As cyber risks evolve, organisations will need to implement new measures to protect their systems and data. Employees who understand the value of security and approach it with a positive mindset will be more open to adapting to these changes and less likely to resist new procedures.

Attitudes are a powerful dimension of security culture. They shape how employees approach security in their daily tasks and play a key role in determining whether secure behaviours will become the norm. By actively fostering positive attitudes through leadership, communication, training, and user-friendly tools, organisations can create a security-conscious workforce that views security not as a burden, but as an integral part of their role in protecting the organisation.

Cognition

Cognition refers to employees' knowledge, understanding, and awareness regarding cybersecurity threats, risks, and best practices. It encompasses the intellectual dimension of security culture, involving an individual's ability to comprehend why security is important, how cyber threats operate, and what actions they must take to protect the organisation from these risks. Simply put, cognition is the mental foundation on which secure behaviour is built.

Without sufficient knowledge of the evolving cyber threat landscape and an understanding of how security policies protect the organisation, employees may struggle to make informed decisions about their actions. Therefore, cognition is a critical dimension in ensuring that employees are not just following security protocols blindly but are actively engaged and informed about why those protocols exist.

A workforce with high levels of security cognition is one that can identify potential risks, understand how to mitigate those risks, and make better decisions in their daily activities. Conversely, poor cognition can lead to unintentional security breaches, as employees may not recognise the warning signs of a phishing attempt, may not understand the risks of weak passwords, or may be unaware of how to securely handle sensitive information.

The Importance of Security Cognition

Cognition forms the intellectual backbone of a strong security culture. It influences both the attitudes and behaviours of employees by providing them with the necessary knowledge and skills to act securely. While attitudes shape how employees feel about security and behaviour shows how they act, cognition is what equips them to make informed, rational decisions in the face of potential threats.

In today's constantly evolving digital landscape, the types of cyber threats facing organisations are becoming increasingly sophisticated. Phishing attacks, social engineering, malware, ransomware, and insider threats all target the human element, seeking to exploit gaps in knowledge or lapses in awareness. A high level of cognition reduces the likelihood of these attacks succeeding because employees are able to recognise the signs of malicious activity and take the appropriate action to prevent a breach.

For example, an employee with high security cognition will understand how to differentiate a legitimate email from a phishing attempt by recognising red flags such as suspicious links, spelling errors, or an unfamiliar sender address. They will also know to report the phishing attempt to the IT or security team, thereby preventing potential harm to the organisation. Conversely, an employee with low cognition may fall victim to the phishing attack, inadvertently compromising sensitive data or giving attackers access to the organisation's systems.

Building Cognition Through Security Awareness Training

The most effective way to improve security cognition across an organisation is through comprehensive and ongoing **security awareness training**. Training provides employees with the knowledge they need to understand the various types of cyber threats and the organisation's security policies, as well as how to respond to potential risks.

However, for training to be effective in building cognition, it must be more than just a one-time exercise. Employees need regular updates and refreshers to stay informed about new threats, changing security policies, and evolving best practices. The cyber threat landscape is always shifting, and without continuous learning, employees may quickly fall behind and become susceptible to emerging attacks.

Effective security awareness training programmes should:

Educate employees on common attack vectors: Phishing, malware, ransomware, and social engineering should be covered in detail, explaining how these threats work and how to recognise them.

Provide practical examples and simulations: Using real-world scenarios, such as mock phishing emails or simulated attacks, helps employees apply their knowledge in a realistic context, improving retention and understanding.

Tailor content to different roles: Training should be role-specific, as different departments may face different kinds of security risks. For example, finance employees may need to focus on protecting financial data and avoiding fraud, while IT staff may need training on preventing system vulnerabilities.

Engage employees with interactive content: Passive training methods, such as long presentations or static documents, may not be effective in building cognition. Instead, interactive content like quizzes, games, and hands-on simulations can significantly enhance engagement and knowledge retention.

Regularly assess knowledge: Quizzes or tests at the end of training modules help ensure employees understand the content. Regular assessments also provide insights into areas where further training may be needed.

Additionally, reinforcing learning with **microlearning** techniques, such as sending brief reminders, tips, or security updates via email or company intranet, can help keep security top-of-mind. This approach ensures that employees regularly engage with security concepts without feeling overwhelmed by long training sessions.

Cognitive Barriers to Security Awareness

While security training is essential for building cognition, organisations often encounter barriers that limit employees' ability to absorb and retain security knowledge. Recognising these barriers is crucial to developing an effective security education programme. Some common cognitive barriers include:

1. **Information Overload**: Employees are often inundated with a vast amount of information in their daily work, and security knowledge can sometimes be lost amid competing priorities. When security messages are too complex or lengthy, they can overwhelm employees, causing them to disengage from the content. Simplifying messages and focusing on core concepts can help mitigate this issue.

2. **Lack of Relevance**: Employees who do not perceive the information as relevant to their roles are less likely to retain it. Generic, one-size-

fits-all training often fails to resonate with individuals whose day-to-day tasks may not obviously connect to security. Tailoring training to different job functions or departments can help make the content more meaningful and relevant, improving engagement and retention.

3. **Cognitive Biases**: Human cognitive biases, such as the **optimism bias** (believing that bad things are less likely to happen to oneself) or **normalcy bias** (believing that future events will unfold as they have in the past), can make employees underestimate the likelihood of a cyber-attack or the consequences of not following security protocols. Addressing these biases in training by using real-life examples and showing the potential impacts of security breaches can help overcome these mental blocks.

4. **Overconfidence**: Some employees may have overconfidence in their knowledge and believe they are unlikely to fall for security threats. Overconfidence can lead to risky behaviours, such as ignoring security alerts or failing to report incidents. Training programmes should show how even experienced, knowledgeable individuals can be tricked by sophisticated attacks, fostering humility and caution.

5. **Resistance to Change**: Employees who are used to certain ways of working may resist adopting new security practices, especially if they perceive them as inconvenient or unnecessary. To address this, security training should clearly explain the reasoning behind security

policies and highlight the risks of maintaining outdated habits. Demonstrating how new practices protect both the organisation and the individual can help reduce resistance.

Measuring Cognition in the Organisation

To understand the level of security cognition within an organisation, it is important to measure and assess employee knowledge regularly. This can be done through several methods:

1. **Knowledge Assessments**: Conducting periodic quizzes or tests following training sessions helps measure employees' understanding of key security concepts. These assessments should cover areas such as identifying phishing emails, recognising social engineering tactics, password management, and understanding the organisation's incident response procedures.

2. **Simulated Attacks**: One of the most effective ways to test security cognition is through phishing simulations or other types of mock attacks. These tests give insight into how well employees can apply their knowledge in real-world situations. The results of these simulations provide valuable data on where employees may need additional training or reinforcement.

3. **Surveys and Feedback**: Employee surveys can offer qualitative insights into how confident individuals feel in their ability to handle

security threats and how well they understand security policies. Surveys also provide an opportunity for employees to offer feedback on the effectiveness of the training they receive, allowing the organisation to make improvements.

4. **Tracking Incidents**: Monitoring the frequency and types of security incidents reported by employees can provide indirect measures of cognition. For example, an increase in the reporting of phishing attempts may indicate that employees are becoming more vigilant and knowledgeable about recognising such threats.

The Long-Term Benefits of Strong Security Cognition

Improving security cognition across the organisation provides long-term benefits that extend beyond immediate security outcomes. Employees with high levels of cognition are more confident in their ability to navigate the complexities of cybersecurity, and this confidence can reduce anxiety and hesitation around engaging with new security measures. Moreover, a knowledgeable workforce is better equipped to handle emerging threats and adapt to evolving security challenges, which enhances the organisation's resilience over time.

Furthermore, security cognition fosters a culture of **shared responsibility**. When employees understand the broader implications of cybersecurity - not just for the organisation but also for themselves personally - they are more likely to take ownership of their role in safeguarding information. This can lead to a more engaged workforce, where security becomes embedded in the daily mindset rather than viewed as a separate, IT-driven concern.

Cognition is a critical security culture dimension that underpins attitudes and behaviour. By investing in continuous education, addressing cognitive barriers, and regularly assessing knowledge, organisations can cultivate a workforce that is not only aware of security threats but also capable of effectively mitigating them. In the long run, strong security cognition creates a proactive, informed, and empowered employee base that actively contributes to the organisation's overall security posture.

Communication

Communication is a critical dimension of security culture, as it encompasses the methods, frequency, clarity, and openness with which security-related information is shared within an organisation. A robust security culture depends on effective communication that ensures employees are consistently informed about security threats, policies, best practices, and their roles in maintaining a secure environment. When communication is clear, timely, and accessible, it empowers employees to take the right actions to protect the organisation.

Conversely, poor communication can lead to confusion, misinformation, and a breakdown in security efforts.

Effective communication is not just about delivering top-down instructions from the security or IT departments; it also involves creating an environment in which security issues are openly discussed, where employees feel comfortable asking questions, and where feedback is actively sought and incorporated into improving security practices. Building a culture of transparent and ongoing communication about cybersecurity is essential for fostering a sense of shared responsibility and vigilance across the organisation.

The Role of Communication in Building Security Culture

Communication is the lifeblood of any organisational initiative, and security is no exception. It is the vehicle through which security policies are conveyed, awareness is raised, and employees are reminded of their obligations. When security communication is well-structured and aligned with the organisation's goals, it strengthens other dimensions of security culture, such as attitudes, cognition, and behaviour.

In organisations where communication is frequent and security messages are embedded into daily workflows, employees are more likely to internalise security practices. These messages might include reminders about password hygiene, updates on new cyber threats, or guidance on reporting security incidents. Frequent and clear communication ensures that security remains a priority for employees rather than a distant concern only addressed during annual training sessions.

On the other hand, poor communication can result in employees being unaware of critical security policies or not understanding why certain measures are necessary. Inconsistent or unclear communication can lead to misunderstandings, misinterpretation of security requirements, and a lack of engagement with security initiatives. This creates gaps in the organisation's defences, as employees may not fully grasp their role in preventing cyber incidents.

Key Elements of Effective Security Communication

Communication must be clear, consistent, timely, and engaging to effectively support a strong security culture. The following elements are critical to ensuring that security communication reaches employees meaningfully.

Clarity and Simplicity for security-related messages should be written in clear, straightforward language that all employees can understand, regardless of their technical expertise. Jargon-heavy or overly complex communications can alienate non-technical staff, making them feel disconnected from security efforts. Simplicity in language ensures that everyone understands the core message, whether they are in finance, human resources, or IT.

When communicating security policies, the focus should be on **what** employees must do and **why** it's important, avoiding unnecessary technical detail. For example, instead of simply instructing employees to update their passwords regularly, explaining how doing so protects both the organisation and their personal information increases the likelihood of compliance.

Consistency is critical in maintaining security awareness over time. Regular communication reinforces key security messages and helps employees remain vigilant against threats. This doesn't mean bombarding employees with constant emails about security, but rather finding a balance where security-related information is provided frequently enough to stay top-of-mind without becoming overwhelming.

Security communication should also be aligned with the organisation's overall messaging and cultural values. If security is only addressed sporadically, employees may perceive it as less important. However, if security is consistently highlighted as a critical part of daily operations, it sends a clear message that it is an integral part of the organisation's values.

Timeliness with communication is crucial, especially when dealing with emerging threats or incidents. For instance, if a new phishing campaign is targeting employees, immediate communication can help raise awareness and prevent an attack from succeeding. Regular updates on security incidents or vulnerabilities that have been identified (both inside and outside the organisation) also demonstrate that the organisation is actively monitoring threats and keeping employees informed.

Timeliness can often mean the difference between a successful and unsuccessful security incident. By providing up-to-date information on threats and security breaches, organisations empower employees to act quickly and appropriately, reducing the risk of widespread damage.

Two-Way Communication is not just top-down. Employees should feel comfortable raising security concerns, asking questions, or seeking clarification when they are unsure about a policy or practice. Creating open communication channels where employees can report suspicious activities or ask for help fosters a culture of trust and mutual responsibility.

Organisations should provide multiple ways for employees to communicate about security, such as designated email addresses for reporting incidents, anonymous feedback forms, or direct contact with the security team. Additionally, encouraging employees to share their experiences or concerns in team meetings can help normalise discussions around security.

Engagement and Relevance to employees are needed for communication to be truly effective. Messages that are dry, overly technical, or disconnected from employees' day-to-day tasks are likely to be ignored or forgotten. Engaging communication techniques, such as storytelling, real-world examples, or interactive formats, can make security messages more memorable and impactful.

Furthermore, security communication should be tailored to different organisational roles and departments. Different teams face different risks - finance departments may need more focus on protecting financial data, while marketing teams may need guidance on securing social media accounts. Organisations can ensure that security messages resonate with employees' responsibilities and interests by making communication relevant to specific roles.

Visual and Multimedia Tools Incorporating visual elements, such as infographics, videos, or flowcharts, can help break down complex security topics and make them more digestible. For example, a short video explaining how to recognise phishing emails or a flowchart outlining the steps to report a security incident can be far more engaging than a lengthy text document.

Multimedia tools can also accommodate different learning styles, making it easier for employees to absorb the information. While some employees may prefer to read policy updates, others may find visual aids or interactive content more effective.

Channels of Security Communication

The medium through which security information is communicated is just as important as the content itself. Organisations need to utilise a variety of channels to ensure that security messages reach employees effectively. Some common channels include:

1. **Email** - Email is one of the most common ways to communicate security updates, tips, and alerts. However, since employees often receive a large volume of emails daily, ensuring that security-related emails stand out is essential. Subject lines should clearly indicate the importance of the message, and the content should be concise and actionable.

While email is effective for regular updates, it should not be the sole method of communication. Employees may miss or overlook important security emails if they are not reinforced through other channels.

2. **Intranet and Collaboration Tools** - Many organisations have internal intranet systems or collaboration platforms (e.g., Microsoft Teams, Slack) where important updates and policies are posted. These

platforms can serve as central hubs for security-related information, providing easy access to policies, training materials, and incident reporting procedures.

Intranet platforms can also host security bulletins or discussion boards where employees can ask questions and stay informed about the latest security trends and threats. Making security information easily accessible on these platforms ensures employees have a go-to resource for any security-related queries.

3. **Face-to-Face or Virtual Meetings** - Regular security briefings, either in-person or through virtual meetings, provide an opportunity for more interactive communication. These sessions allow for real-time Q&A, discussion of specific security concerns, and deeper dives into complex topics. Security teams can present case studies of recent incidents, share insights from security audits, or provide updates on new policies.

Face-to-face communication also offers the added benefit of personal engagement, which can be more effective than written communication alone in building trust and reinforcing the importance of security.

4. **Posters and Visual Reminders** - Physical reminders in the workplace, such as posters or digital signage, can serve as constant, passive reinforcements of security messages. Simple reminders like

"Lock your computer before you leave your desk" or "Report suspicious emails" placed in high-traffic areas can help reinforce secure behaviours without being intrusive.

Visual reminders can be particularly effective when employees do not regularly engage with digital communication, such as warehouses or field offices.

5. **Push Notifications and Alerts** - Push notifications or pop-up alerts can effectively disseminate urgent security information quickly. For example, if a new phishing campaign is detected targeting the organisation, a pop-up alert on employee computers or a push notification to their phones can serve as an immediate warning, helping to prevent a potential breach.

However, these alerts should be used sparingly to avoid overwhelming employees or creating a sense of "alert fatigue," where frequent notifications are ignored.

The Importance of Leadership in Security Communication

Leadership plays a vital role in setting the tone for security communication within the organisation. When leaders actively engage in security efforts and consistently communicate the importance of cybersecurity, it sends a powerful message to employees that security is a priority. Leadership's commitment to security should be visible through their participation in security training, adherence to security policies, and regular communication about the organisation's security goals.

Executives and managers should also be involved in communicating the impact of security on the broader business strategy. When employees understand that security is integral to the organisation's success - not just an IT concern - they are more likely to take security seriously. Leaders who model secure behaviour and encourage open communication about security concerns help foster a culture of trust and accountability.

Measuring the Effectiveness of Security Communication

Organisations should regularly assess how well security messages are received and understood by employees to ensure effective communication. This can be achieved through:

1. **Surveys and Feedback**: Asking employees for feedback on security communication can provide valuable insights into what is working and what needs improvement. Surveys can measure whether employees feel informed about security policies, understand their roles, and feel confident in reporting incidents.

2. **Knowledge Assessments**: Quizzes or tests following security training can assess how well employees have absorbed the information. These assessments can identify gaps in understanding that may need to be addressed through additional communication.

3. **Tracking Incident Reports**: Monitoring how frequently employees report suspicious activity or security incidents can provide indirect insights into communication effectiveness. If incident reporting is low, it may indicate that employees are unaware of reporting procedures or feel uncomfortable raising concerns.

4. **Engagement Metrics**: Tracking engagement with security communication channels - such as email open rates, intranet visits, or attendance at security briefings - - can help measure how actively employees are engaging with security messages. Low engagement may suggest that communication needs to be more engaging or relevant.

Communication is the glue that holds an organisation's security culture together. Without clear, consistent, and open communication, even the best security policies and technologies will fail to achieve their full potential. By ensuring that security messages are accessible, engaging, and relevant to employees, organisations can create a culture where security is a shared responsibility and where employees feel empowered to act as the first line of defence.

A strong communication strategy not only enhances security awareness but also builds trust, ensuring that employees feel comfortable raising concerns and asking questions. Over time, effective communication helps to reinforce positive security attitudes and behaviours, creating a more resilient and secure organisation.

Compliance

Compliance, as a dimension of security culture, refers to the degree to which employees adhere to the organisation's security policies, procedures, and regulations. While compliance is often seen as the baseline for security culture, it plays a pivotal role in ensuring that the organisation meets both internal and external security requirements, including legal, regulatory, and industry-specific standards. Compliance serves as a safeguard, ensuring that employees follow established guidelines designed to protect the organisation from cyber threats, data breaches, and security incidents.

In essence, compliance is about following the rules. But for compliance to be effective, it must go beyond simply enforcing security policies through penalties or audits - it should be embedded in the everyday actions and mindsets of employees. When employees understand the reasons behind security policies and are motivated to comply not only out of obligation but also out of a genuine commitment to protecting the organisation, compliance becomes a natural part of the organisational culture.

The Importance of Compliance in Security Culture

Compliance is crucial for maintaining a strong security posture within any organisation. It ensures that all employees, regardless of their role or department, are following the same set of security protocols, thus creating consistency in how security is approached. This standardisation is particularly important in large, decentralised organisations where different teams or regions might otherwise develop their own interpretations of security practices.

At a higher level, compliance is often required by law or industry standards. Regulations such as the General Data Protection Regulation (GDPR), the Health Insurance Portability and Accountability Act (HIPAA), the Payment Card Industry Data Security Standard (PCI DSS), and various ISO standards mandate strict security protocols to protect personal and sensitive data. Failing to comply with these regulations can result in severe penalties, reputational damage, and a loss of customer trust. For businesses operating in highly regulated industries like finance, healthcare, or government, compliance with these standards is non-negotiable.

However, compliance is not just about avoiding fines or meeting regulatory requirements. It also directly contributes to reducing the risk of cyber threats. By ensuring that employees consistently follow security procedures - such as encrypting data, using multi-factor authentication

(MFA), and regularly updating software - organisations are better equipped to defend against external attacks and internal vulnerabilities. Compliance, therefore, plays a dual role: it protects the organisation from legal and regulatory risks while also strengthening its resilience against cyber threats.

Key Elements of Effective Compliance

For compliance to effectively contribute to security culture, it needs to be comprehensive, practical, and well-communicated. Here are the key elements of effective compliance in security culture.

Clear and Understandable Policies - The foundation of compliance is having clear, accessible, and understandable security policies. Employees must know exactly what is expected of them, and these expectations should be outlined in a way that is easy to follow. Security policies should avoid overly technical jargon and instead focus on what employees need to do to stay compliant with security requirements.

Policies should cover all critical areas of security, such as:

- Data protection and privacy measures (e.g., encrypting sensitive data, proper data storage, and handling practices).
- Password management protocols (e.g., using strong, unique passwords, and implementing MFA).

- Device and endpoint security (e.g., locking workstations, securing mobile devices, and avoiding the use of unauthorised software).

- Incident reporting and response procedures (e.g., how to report phishing attempts or suspected breaches).

Clear policies ensure that employees are not confused about what is required, reducing the risk of non-compliance due to misunderstanding.

Regular Training and Awareness - Compliance must be reinforced through regular training and awareness campaigns. Employees need to be continuously educated on new security policies, regulatory updates, and emerging threats that may affect their compliance obligations. Training should be engaging and tailored to the specific needs of different teams and roles within the organisation.

Security awareness training helps employees understand not only **how** to comply with security policies but also **why** compliance is necessary. For example, employees should be made aware of the potential consequences of non-compliance, such as data breaches, financial penalties, and reputational harm. By reinforcing the importance of compliance in protecting both the organisation and its customers, employees are more likely to take compliance seriously.

Furthermore, compliance training should be provided regularly, not just as a one-time exercise. This ensures that employees stay up-to-date on new threats, evolving regulations, and changes to internal policies. Regular refresher courses help to keep compliance top-of-mind, reducing the likelihood of lapses due to forgetfulness or complacency.

Monitoring and Auditing - An essential aspect of compliance is the ability to monitor, measure, and audit adherence to security policies. Monitoring ensures that employees consistently follow security protocols, while regular audits help identify areas where compliance may be lacking. These audits should cover various aspects of security, including password management, data encryption practices, incident response times, and adherence to industry-specific regulations.

Monitoring tools, such as automated compliance tracking systems, can help organisations identify gaps in compliance in real time. For example, suppose employees are not regularly updating their software or using unauthorised devices. In that case, these tools can flag the issue, allowing the organisation to take corrective action before a potential security breach occurs.

Audits also play a crucial role in compliance with external regulations. Many regulations, such as GDPR or PCI DSS, require organisations to demonstrate that they are following specific security protocols. Regular internal and external audits help ensure that the organisation is prepared to pass regulatory inspections and avoid fines or penalties for non-compliance.

Enforcement and Accountability - While compliance should ideally be driven by employee engagement and understanding, there must also be clear consequences for failing to follow security policies. Organisations need to establish a system of enforcement that holds employees accountable for non-compliance. This does not necessarily mean punitive measures for every minor infraction, but there should be clear escalation procedures for repeated or deliberate violations.

A strong enforcement framework includes:

- **Clear reporting lines** for security incidents or non-compliance, ensuring that employees know how and where to report issues.

- **Defined disciplinary measures** for repeated non-compliance, such as retraining, warnings, or, in severe cases, termination of employment.

- **Positive reinforcement**, such as recognising and rewarding employees who consistently follow security protocols, which can create a culture of accountability through positive incentives.

The goal of enforcement is not to create a culture of fear but to ensure that employees take compliance seriously and understand the importance of adhering to security policies.

Leadership Commitment - Leadership must champion compliance for it to become an integral part of the organisation's security culture. When leaders consistently follow and promote security policies, they set an example for the rest of the organisation. If leaders disregard security protocols, they send a message that compliance is not a priority, which can lead to widespread non-compliance among employees.

Leadership should also communicate the importance of compliance during meetings, presentations, and company-wide communications. By demonstrating their own commitment to following security policies, leaders can help create a culture where compliance is seen as an essential part of the organisation's success, rather than a burdensome requirement.

The Challenges of Achieving Compliance

While compliance is fundamental to security culture, achieving it consistently can be challenging. Several factors can make compliance difficult for organisations, particularly when security policies are seen as overly complex or disruptive to employees' daily workflows.

Understanding these challenges can help organisations develop strategies to overcome them.

Complex or Inconvenient Policies - One of the most common reasons for non-compliance is that security policies are perceived as too complex or inconvenient. For example, requiring employees to change their passwords frequently or using cumbersome multi-factor authentication systems can lead to frustration, causing employees to bypass security measures or find workarounds.

To address this, organisations should strive to simplify their security policies and make compliance as easy as possible. User-friendly security tools, streamlined processes, and a focus on reducing the burden on employees can all help improve compliance rates. The key is to balance security needs with usability, ensuring that compliance does not come at the expense of employee productivity.

Lack of Awareness or Understanding - Employees may not fully understand the importance of compliance or may be unaware of the specific policies they are required to follow. This is particularly common in organisations with complex regulatory requirements, where employees may feel overwhelmed by the sheer volume of security protocols.

Addressing this challenge requires effective communication and training. Employees need to be educated not just on the policies but also on why they exist. When employees understand how their actions impact the overall security of the organisation, they are more likely to comply with security policies out of a sense of responsibility rather than obligation.

Resistance to Change - Employees may resist new security policies or changes to existing protocols, particularly if they feel that the changes disrupt their established workflows. This resistance is often rooted in a lack of understanding of the reasons behind the changes or a perception that the new policies are unnecessary.

To overcome this, organisations should involve employees in the process of implementing new security policies. Engaging employees in discussions about the need for change, seeking their feedback, and providing clear explanations of the benefits of new policies can help reduce resistance and improve buy-in.

Geographically Dispersed Teams - In global organisations, ensuring consistent compliance across different regions can be challenging. Different countries may have varying regulatory requirements, and cultural differences can influence how security policies are perceived and followed.

To manage this challenge, organisations need to ensure that security policies are flexible enough to accommodate local regulations while maintaining a consistent approach to compliance. Regular communication and coordination between global and regional security teams are essential to ensure that all employees, regardless of location, are aware of and adhering to the organisation's security requirements.

Measuring Compliance

To assess the effectiveness of compliance within the organisation, it is important to establish clear metrics and regularly measure adherence to security policies. Key performance indicators (KPIs) for compliance might include:

- **Policy Adherence Rates**: The percentage of employees following security policies, such as regularly changing passwords or encrypting sensitive data.

- **Completion of Training**: Tracking how many employees have completed required security training modules and whether they have passed assessments or quizzes.

- **Incident Reporting Rates**: Monitoring the frequency with which employees report potential security incidents, such as phishing attempts or suspicious activity.

- **Audit Results**: Results from internal and external security audits, which can provide insights into how well the organisation is complying with industry standards and regulations.

By regularly reviewing these metrics, organisations can identify areas where compliance may be lacking and take corrective action.

Compliance is an essential component of security culture, providing a foundation for consistent, standardised security practices across the organisation. While regulatory requirements often drive compliance, its true value lies in reducing cyber risk and creating a more secure working environment. By ensuring that security policies are clear, practical, and supported by training, monitoring, and leadership, organisations can foster a culture where compliance is seen not as a burden, but as an integral part of protecting the business.

In a strong security culture, compliance is not just about following rules - it is about understanding the importance of those rules and taking proactive steps to protect the organisation from cyber threats. Over time, a commitment to compliance can significantly enhance the organisation's resilience to cyberattacks, data breaches, and other security incidents, helping safeguard the business and its stakeholders.

Norms

Norms, as a dimension of security culture, refer to the unwritten rules and informal expectations that guide employees' behaviour within an organisation. These shared beliefs about what constitutes acceptable or expected behaviour are often shaped by social influence, peer actions, and the broader organisational culture. Unlike formal policies or procedures, norms are typically not explicitly documented, yet they significantly influence how employees approach security practices.

In many ways, norms are the invisible force determining whether employees will follow security protocols, report incidents, or engage in secure behaviour daily. They are established over time through repeated behaviours and collective attitudes, and they can either support or undermine formal security policies. When security norms align with the organisation's security goals, employees are more likely to engage in secure practices voluntarily. However, if norms are misaligned - such as a culture where taking security shortcuts is common - this can lead to widespread non-compliance and increased risk.

Understanding and shaping security norms is critical to building a strong security culture. Norms create the behavioural "default settings" that employees turn to, especially in situations where they are unsure how to act or when formal policies are unclear. A strong security culture requires cultivating norms that encourage and reinforce secure behaviour as part of everyday work life.

The Role of Norms in Security Culture

Norms profoundly influence employee behaviour because they provide a sense of social expectations within the organisation. People tend to conform to what they perceive as the standard or accepted way of doing things, especially in environments with a strong desire to fit in or avoid standing out negatively. This is particularly true when it comes to security, where employees may look to their peers to gauge the level of vigilance required.

For example, in an organisation where it is the norm to lock computers before leaving desks, employees are likelier to follow this behaviour because they see their peers doing the same. On the other hand, if employees observe their colleagues regularly bypassing security protocols - such as ignoring email security warnings or sharing passwords - it signals that such behaviour is acceptable, even if it violates formal policies. Over time, these norms can either strengthen or erode the organisation's security posture.

In a positive security culture, norms reinforce formal policies by creating a shared understanding that security is everyone's responsibility. Employees in these organisations feel a sense of accountability to follow security protocols and encourage their peers to do the same. This creates an environment where secure behaviour becomes a collective norm, rather than something driven solely by top-down enforcement.

How Norms Develop

Norms develop over time as a result of both formal and informal influences. Several factors contribute to the establishment of security norms within an organisation.

Leadership Influence - Leaders play a crucial role in shaping norms by setting the tone for security culture. When executives and managers consistently follow security protocols and emphasise their importance, they send a strong message to employees that security is a priority. For example, if leadership is diligent about locking their computers, using strong passwords, and participating in security training, these actions help establish secure behaviours as the norm throughout the organisation.

Conversely, when leaders disregard security protocols or fail to model secure behaviour, it can signal to employees that security is not important. This can result in a culture where shortcuts and risky behaviours become the norm, undermining the organisation's security efforts.

Peer Influence and Social Proof - Employees often look to their peers to determine acceptable behaviour, especially when there is ambiguity about the correct course of action. This concept of **social proof -** the idea that people conform to the actions of others in an attempt to reflect correct behaviour - is a powerful driver of norms.

For instance, in an open-plan office environment, if most employees habitually lock their computers when leaving their desks, others will likely adopt this behaviour. Similarly, if employees observe their colleagues reporting phishing emails or following proper password management practices, these behaviours are more likely to become embedded in the organisation's norms.

Social influence also extends to how employees react to security violations. In a culture where employees hold each other accountable - such as gently reminding colleagues to lock their screens - norms are reinforced through peer interactions. This creates a positive feedback loop that encourages compliance with security best practices.

Past Experiences - Employees' past experiences with security incidents, breaches, or threats also play a role in shaping norms. If an organisation has experienced a serious security breach, it can lead to a heightened awareness of security risks, resulting in a shift in norms towards more vigilant behaviour. For example, employees who have witnessed or been affected by a phishing attack are more likely to adopt secure behaviours, such as being cautious about email links or reporting suspicious messages.

On the other hand, employees may become complacent if an organisation has never experienced a significant security incident or if incidents are not widely communicated. Without a clear understanding of the risks, insecure behaviours may become normalised.

Organisational Culture and Values - The broader organisational culture and its underlying values influence security norms. In organisations where accountability, transparency, and risk management are core values, secure behaviours are more likely to be embraced as part of the organisational identity. In contrast, in organisations where speed, convenience, or innovation are prioritised over caution and diligence, employees may tend to take shortcuts that compromise security.

Aligning security with the organisation's core values is crucial for embedding security into the culture. For example, if the organisation values collaboration, then fostering norms around securely sharing information and working together to prevent security incidents becomes important. Likewise, if innovation is a key value, promoting secure innovation - such as ensuring that new technologies or processes are securely implemented - helps reinforce positive security norms.

Positive vs. Negative Security Norms

Norms can either support or undermine an organisation's security culture. Understanding the difference between positive and negative security norms is critical for organisations that aim to strengthen their security practices.

Positive Security Norms - Positive security norms align with the organisation's security policies and encourage employees to engage in secure behaviour. These norms promote a culture of shared responsibility, where employees are aware of security risks and actively take steps to mitigate them. Examples of positive security norms include:

- Locking computers when leaving workstations.

- Regularly updating passwords and using password managers.

- Reporting suspicious emails or potential security incidents promptly.

- Following data protection practices, such as encrypting sensitive information.

- Participating in security awareness training and staying informed about the latest threats.

In organisations with strong positive norms, security becomes an ingrained part of daily operations. Employees don't need to be constantly reminded to follow protocols because secure behaviour is the "default" and is reinforced through both peer influence and leadership.

Negative Security Norms - Negative security norms, on the other hand, undermine security efforts by normalising risky behaviours or non-compliance. These norms may develop when employees perceive security protocols as inconvenient, unnecessary, or overly restrictive. Examples of negative security norms include:

- Sharing passwords with colleagues or writing them down in unsecured locations.

- Ignoring security alerts or warnings because they are seen as disruptive.

- Using unauthorised personal devices for work-related tasks without proper security measures.

- Bypassing security procedures, such as skipping multi-factor authentication (MFA), to save time.

Negative norms can spread quickly in an organisation, especially if leadership fails to address them. Once risky behaviours become normalised, they can be difficult to reverse, increasing the likelihood of security breaches or incidents.

Shaping and Reinforcing Positive Security Norms

For organisations aiming to strengthen their security culture, actively shaping and reinforcing positive security norms is essential. While formal policies provide the framework for secure behaviour, norms ensure that these policies are consistently followed in practice. Here are several strategies for promoting positive security norms.

Lead by Example - Leadership's role in shaping norms cannot be overstated. Leaders must consistently model secure behaviour, such as following security policies, participating in training, and communicating the importance of security. When employees see their leaders taking security seriously, they are more likely to follow suit.

Leadership can also set expectations for how security should be approached within teams, reinforcing that security is not just the IT department's responsibility but everyone in the organisation. By making security a visible priority, leaders help embed secure behaviours into the organisational norms.

Encourage Peer Accountability - Creating a culture of peer accountability, where employees feel comfortable reminding each other about security practices, can reinforce positive norms. For example, encouraging employees to gently remind a colleague to lock their computer when stepping away helps build a sense of collective responsibility for security.

Peer accountability can also be promoted through formal mechanisms, such as establishing **Security Champions** in different departments. These champions act as role models and advocates for secure behaviour, helping to influence and shape the norms within their teams.

Normalise Secure Behaviour Through Communication - Regular and transparent communication about security helps reinforce norms by keeping security top-of-mind for employees. For example, sharing success stories about how following security protocols prevented a potential breach can highlight the importance of secure behaviour. Similarly, reporting on incidents or near misses while maintaining confidentiality can raise awareness of the consequences of lax security practices.

Security-related communications should also focus on making secure behaviour seem routine and normal. Instead of framing security policies as exceptional or burdensome, they should be presented as a natural part of doing business.

Reward and Recognise Secure Behaviour - Recognising and rewarding employees who consistently demonstrate secure behaviour can help reinforce positive norms. Public recognition, such as naming "Security Champions of the Month" or offering incentives for employees who report phishing attempts, can encourage others to adopt similar behaviours.

Positive reinforcement is an effective way to make secure behaviour desirable, not just required. Organisations can gradually shift norms toward more proactive security practices by celebrating small wins.

Address Negative Norms Proactively - When negative norms begin to emerge, it's crucial to address them quickly and effectively. If employees frequently bypass security protocols, such as ignoring MFA prompts or using unsecured devices, leadership must intervene to understand the root cause and implement solutions. This might involve simplifying security processes, providing additional training, or reinforcing the consequences of non-compliance.

Formal enforcement measures may sometimes be necessary to address widespread non-compliance. However, these should be balanced with efforts to engage employees and understand why negative norms have developed in the first place.

Measuring and Monitoring Norms

While norms are inherently informal and difficult to quantify directly, organisations can assess the presence of positive or negative security norms through several methods:

1. **Employee Surveys**: Surveys can provide insights into how employees perceive security and whether they feel that secure behaviours are the norm within their teams. Questions might focus on how often employees see their peers following security protocols, whether they feel comfortable reporting security incidents, or how strongly they believe leadership supports security efforts.

2. **Incident Reporting**: Monitoring the frequency and quality of incident reporting can indicate the presence of positive security norms. In organisations where secure behaviour is the norm, employees are more likely to report security threats, near misses, or suspicious activity promptly.

3. **Security Audits**: Regular security audits can reveal patterns of behaviour that suggest the presence of positive or negative norms. For example, suppose an audit shows that a significant number of employees are using weak passwords or ignoring software updates. In that case, it may indicate that negative norms around password hygiene have developed.

4. **Observation**: Direct observation of employee behaviour, such as how often employees lock their computers or whether they use secure methods to share information, can provide valuable insights into an organisation's norms. This can be done informally or through more structured methods, such as mystery audits or security assessments.

Norms are a powerful but often overlooked dimension of security culture. They shape how employees behave in practice, influencing whether they comply with security policies, report incidents, or take shortcuts that increase risk. By actively shaping and reinforcing positive security norms, organisations can create an environment where secure behaviour is the default and where employees feel a shared responsibility for protecting the organisation from cyber threats.

Cultivating positive norms requires a combination of leadership, communication, peer influence, and reinforcement. By embedding secure behaviour into the everyday fabric of organisational life, companies can significantly enhance their security culture and reduce the likelihood of breaches caused by human error or non-compliance.

Responsibilities

As a dimension of security culture, responsibilities refer to the clear definition and understanding of roles and duties regarding cybersecurity within an organisation. In a strong security culture, everyone - from the boardroom to the frontlines - has a defined role to play in maintaining and enhancing the organisation's security posture. While the IT and security teams may hold the technical reins, a culture of shared responsibility ensures that all employees are aware of their individual contributions to protecting the organisation from cyber threats.

Security responsibilities extend beyond simply following policies and procedures; they also encompass proactive engagement with security initiatives, reporting suspicious activities, and continuously updating one's own awareness of cybersecurity risks. When employees understand their specific security responsibilities, they are more likely to take ownership of their role in maintaining a secure environment.

A security culture based on shared responsibility encourages accountability at all levels of the organisation. It fosters a sense of ownership where security is seen not just as the concern of IT departments but as a collective effort involving all employees. This chapter explores the importance of defining and communicating security responsibilities, how different roles contribute to the security posture, and the strategies organisations can use to foster a culture of accountability.

The Importance of Defining Responsibilities

Clearly defined security responsibilities are critical for ensuring that employees understand their role in the organisation's overall security framework. Without clear responsibilities, employees may either assume that security is not their concern or, conversely, may feel uncertain about what specific actions they should be taking to contribute to a secure environment.

When responsibilities are unclear, it can lead to significant gaps in the organisation's security defences. For example, employees may not know when or how to report suspicious activities, resulting in delayed responses to potential threats. Similarly, if managers and team leaders are not aware of their role in promoting security awareness, their teams may not receive the necessary guidance and support to follow security best practices.

Clear security responsibilities also help to align employees' actions with the organisation's broader security goals. Each employee should know how their specific role impacts the security posture, whether they are handling sensitive data, managing IT systems, or engaging with external partners. By defining responsibilities, organisations ensure that security becomes a part of every employee's day-to-day activities, not just a compliance checkbox.

Creating a Culture of Accountability

For security responsibilities to be effective, they must be accompanied by a sense of accountability at all levels of the organisation. Creating a culture of accountability involves more than assigning tasks; it requires fostering an environment where individuals feel responsible for their role in maintaining security and understand the consequences of failing to meet their responsibilities.

Here are some strategies to build accountability into a security culture.

Clear Communication One of the most important aspects of fostering accountability is communicating responsibilities. Employees at all levels should understand what is expected of them and why their role is essential to the organisation's overall security efforts. Regular communication from leadership and managers reinforces these expectations and helps ensure that security remains a priority.

Training and Support Employees must have the knowledge and tools necessary to fulfil their security responsibilities. This includes regular security awareness training, clear guidance on following security protocols, and access to support when needed. When employees feel empowered to fulfil their responsibilities, they are more likely to take ownership of their role in maintaining security.

Incentives and Recognition Positive reinforcement can be a powerful motivator for fostering accountability. Recognising and rewarding employees or teams who consistently demonstrate secure behaviour helps reinforce the message that security is valued and expected. Incentives, such as public recognition, awards, or tangible rewards, can encourage others to follow suit and take their security responsibilities seriously.

Enforcement of Consequences While positive reinforcement is essential, there must also be consequences for failing to meet security responsibilities. This could range from additional training for employees who inadvertently bypass security protocols to more serious disciplinary actions for deliberate or repeated violations. By clearly outlining the consequences of non-compliance, organisations create a framework where accountability is taken seriously.

Leadership by Example Accountability starts at the top. When leadership models responsible behaviour and takes their own security obligations seriously, it sets a precedent for the rest of the organisation. Leaders must follow security policies and hold themselves accountable to the same standards they expect from employees.

Measuring and Monitoring Responsibilities

Organisations should regularly assess how well employees are meeting their security obligations to ensure that security responsibilities are being effectively carried out. This can be done through a variety of methods, including:

1. **Performance Reviews** Including security-related metrics in employee performance reviews helps ensure that security responsibilities are

taken seriously. For example, employees might be evaluated on their compliance with security protocols, their engagement with security training, or their role in reporting incidents.

2. **Security Audits** Regular audits can assess whether security responsibilities are being fulfilled at both the individual and departmental levels. Audits may include reviewing how well security policies are followed, assessing the effectiveness of incident reporting procedures, or checking for gaps in compliance.

3. **Incident Reporting and Analysis** Tracking the number and type of security incidents employees report provides insights into how well individuals are fulfilling their responsibility to stay vigilant. Organisations can use this data to identify trends, assess areas for improvement, and provide targeted support or training where necessary.

4. **Feedback Mechanisms** Gathering feedback from employees on their understanding of their security responsibilities can help organisations identify gaps in communication or training. Regular surveys or feedback forms can provide valuable insights into whether employees feel confident in fulfilling their roles and where additional guidance may be needed.

Responsibilities are a crucial dimension of security culture, as they ensure that every individual within the organisation understands their role in maintaining security. From the executive leadership team to frontline employees, each person has a part in protecting the organisation from cyber threats. By clearly defining, communicating, and reinforcing these responsibilities, organisations can build a culture where security is a shared effort and accountability is embraced at all levels.

A strong security culture is one where employees take ownership of their security responsibilities, feel empowered to act, and understand the broader impact of their actions on the organisation's security posture. Through leadership, communication, training, and reinforcement, organisations can foster a culture of responsibility that significantly enhances their resilience to cyber threats and ensures that security is integrated into every aspect of the business.

Building a Strong Security Culture

Building and maintaining a strong security culture requires a multi-dimensional approach that addresses each of these seven areas. Organisations should start by assessing their current culture and identifying strengths and weaknesses in each dimension. From there, a tailored strategy can be developed to strengthen the areas that need improvement.

Leadership commitment is crucial to success. When leaders champion security, it signals to the entire organisation that it is a priority. Regular training, clear communication, and visible support for security initiatives help embed secure behaviours and attitudes throughout the workforce.

Finally, continuous improvement is key. Security threats evolve, and so too must the organisation's approach to security culture. Regular reviews of each dimension ensure that the culture remains strong and adaptable to new challenges.

Security culture is not a one-size-fits-all solution. Each organisation has its unique context, and developing a robust security culture requires addressing the seven dimensions of behaviour, attitudes, cognition, communication, compliance, norms, and responsibilities. By focusing on these areas, organisations can create an environment where security is woven into the fabric of daily operations, reducing risk and enhancing resilience against cyber threats.

Chapter 6

The Global Organisation

In today's interconnected world, a global organisation must navigate a complex tapestry of cultural, legal, and societal norms to develop an effective, resilient security strategy. The proliferation of cyber threats does not respect geographical boundaries, making understanding cultural diversity in security practices paramount. As we delve into the intricacies of securing global enterprises, it's crucial to recognise that what works in one region might be less effective in another. This chapter aims to provide a comprehensive overview of how various regions - North America, Europe, Asia, Latin America, Africa, the Middle East, and

Australia - approach security, highlighting the necessity for a flexible, informed strategy that respects and utilises cultural differences to bolster global security posture.

Cultural diversity significantly influences security practices around the globe. For instance, the European regulatory environment, shaped by initiatives like the General Data Protection Regulation (GDPR), emphasises privacy and data protection, shaping the security strategies businesses must adopt. In contrast, Asian countries may emphasise hierarchical, collective values, affecting how security policies are embraced and executed at all levels of an organisation. Understanding these regional nuances allows global organisations to craft security strategies compliant with local regulations and aligned with cultural values, ensuring greater adherence and effectiveness. It highlights the critical balance between global standardisation and regional adaptation, fostering an environment where employees feel culturally understood and engaged in the security culture.

Beyond compliance and cultural alignment, fostering a globally coherent security culture requires ongoing communication, education, and training tailored to each region's unique challenges and threats. Engaging local stakeholders as champions for security within their communities can bridge gaps between corporate security policy and local practices. This approach demystifies security for a diverse workforce and leverages local insights to strengthen global security frameworks. As global organisations embark on this journey, the goal remains clear: to weave a tight-knit fabric of security-conscious cultures worldwide, resilient in the face of evolving cyber threats. This chapter offers guidance on achieving this by respecting cultural diversity as a cornerstone of a robust global security strategy.

Cultural Diversity in Security Practices

In our interconnected world, the 'global organisation' concept is no longer confined to multinational corporations but extends to businesses of all sizes that operate internationally. The imperative need to address and incorporate cultural diversity in security practices is at the heart of this global operation. Given the complexity and variety of threats businesses face today, understanding and integrating diverse cultural approaches to security isn't just beneficial; it's essential for resilience.

Cultural diversity profoundly impacts security practices. Each culture brings its perceptions of risk, attitudes towards authority, and ways of communicating, all of which need careful consideration when implementing a global security strategy. For instance, the directness in communication favoured in North American cultures can be quite different from the more nuanced approaches in many Asian cultures.

These differences can significantly affect how security policies and practices are perceived, understood, and executed across global teams.

Moreover, leadership styles and the importance placed on hierarchy vary significantly across cultures. Countries with a high Power Distance Index (PDI), like many found in the Middle East and Asia, may require security policies that are more directive, coming from the top down, whereas cultures with a low PDI, such as those in Scandinavia, might favour a more collaborative and consultative approach. Recognising and adapting to these leadership and hierarchical nuances is critical in fostering a security-conscious organisational culture.

Attitudes towards technology and innovation in security practices are another area affected by cultural diversity. In some cultures, there is a strong inclination to adopt the latest technological advancements for security enhancements, while in others, there may be scepticism or a preference for traditional methods. This divergence not only influences the adoption rate of security technologies but also impacts the training and educational initiatives necessary for implementing these technologies effectively.

The first step towards integrating cultural diversity into security practices involves conducting thorough cultural assessments. These assessments can identify potential cultural barriers or facilitators to effective security measures and help tailor communication and education programmes that resonate across different cultural contexts. Such bespoke approaches ensure that all organisation members, regardless of their cultural background, are engaged and committed to the collective security mission.

Engaging local leadership and champions within each region or country is also vital. These individuals can act as cultural brokers, interpreting and adapting global security policies in culturally congruent ways. Their deep understanding of local norms, values, and practices allows for more nuanced and effective implementation of security strategies, enhancing overall compliance and resilience.

In summary, integrating cultural diversity into security practices is not optional but a foundational aspect of developing a truly global, resilient, and secure organisation. By embracing and tailoring approaches to suit varied cultural contexts, businesses can ensure their security practices are as robust and adaptable as the global landscape in which they operate. Such cultural sensitivity strengthens security posture and fosters a more inclusive and unified organisational culture.

In our increasingly globalised world, security threats have become more complex and multifaceted. As organisations extend their operations across various regions, grasping the nuances of local geographic cultures is crucial for crafting effective security strategies. The following pages offer a cultural overview by continent.

North America

When traversing the complex landscape of security practices worldwide, the narrative inevitably turns towards North America, a region that arguably sets the pace for technological advancement and its corresponding security challenges and innovations. Leaders need to grasp the unique cultural and operational aspects that shape the approach to security within this diverse and technologically advanced region.

The emphasis here is on the confluence of innovation, culture, and regulation that drives the security outlook in North America. Unlike other regions where regulatory frameworks might lag technological advancements, North America, particularly the United States and Canada, often leads with regulations that aim to address security concerns preemptively, sometimes setting a precedent for global security standards. This proactivity stems from a culture deeply ingrained with a sense of individual liberty, which paradoxically demands robust privacy protections while fostering an open innovation environment.

Understanding the North American approach to security also means appreciating the role of cross-sector collaborations. Public-private partnerships are a cornerstone of the North American security ecosystem, facilitating a dynamic exchange of intelligence and best practices that bolster the private sector's and the public's resilience against threats. These collaborative efforts have led to the most innovative security solutions and practices worldwide.

Moreover, the leadership role that North American businesses play in the global economy can't be understated. With many multinational corporations headquartered in the US and Canada, the security strategies employed here often have a ripple effect, influencing security postures in subsidiaries and business partners worldwide. Thus, cultivating a security-conscious culture within North American enterprises is about local or national resilience and uplifting global security standards.

However, this leadership position comes with its own set of challenges. The pace of technological adoption means that businesses and security leaders must constantly anticipate new vulnerabilities and threats, embodying a state of perpetual vigilance and adaptation. It requires an organisational culture where security is seen not as a compliance obligation but as a foundational business enabler - a principle that underpins the most successful North American enterprises.

For leaders striving to foster a security-conscious organisation, taking a cue from North America's proactive, collaborative, and culture-centric approach can provide valuable insights. It's about striking the right balance between leveraging technological advancements for competitive advantage while mitigating the risks those same technologies might introduce. It's a dynamic, challenging environment, but with the right mindset, strategies, and practices, it's also one teeming with opportunities to elevate security to new heights.

Europe

Europe encompasses a rich and diverse tapestry of cultures, each presenting unique challenges and opportunities for developing a robust security-conscious organisation. In navigating these intricacies, leaders play pivotal roles in bridging the gap between diverse cultural landscapes and implementing effective, resilient cybersecurity practices.

Understanding and appreciating cultural dimensions is crucial in the European context. For example, Hofstede's cultural dimensions theory provides a valuable framework for dissecting the cultural factors influencing perceptions of security and risk. European countries vary significantly on scales of individualism versus collectivism, uncertainty avoidance, and power distance. These variations reflect organisations' readiness to adopt security measures, report incidents, and comply with security policies.

For instance, Northern European cultures, with their high score on individualism, may emphasise personal responsibility towards cybersecurity. In contrast, Southern European cultures, which may score higher in uncertainty avoidance, could prefer more structured and clear guidelines on security practices. Therefore, crafting a security-conscious organisation in Europe requires a bespoke approach that considers these cultural nuances.

Leadership within European organisations must embody the principles of a resilient security culture. This involves the top-down enforcement of security measures and fostering an environment where security is everyone's responsibility. It's about creating a dialogue, encouraging openness, and ensuring all members feel valued and understood, regardless of their cultural background.

Engaging and motivating employees across Europe also necessitates an approach tailored to diverse cultural sensibilities. Educational initiatives and training programmes must be sensitive to linguistic differences and employ relevant, culturally resonant examples. Furthermore, leveraging local Security Champions can significantly enhance the effectiveness of security awareness efforts, providing a relatable point of reference for team members and facilitating deeper engagement with security practices.

Finally, integrating technological solutions with cultural initiatives demands careful consideration in Europe. The variegated landscape of data protection regulations, such as the GDPR, adds another layer of complexity to deploying technology in service of security. Best practices for technology deployment in Europe emphasise transparency, respect for privacy, and compliance with local and regional regulations.

Building a security-conscious organisation in Europe is a multifaceted endeavour beyond mere compliance or implementing technical solutions. It's about weaving security into the fabric of the organisation's culture, acknowledging and celebrating diversity, and engaging in continuous dialogue to adapt to an ever-changing threat landscape. For leaders, the journey towards resilience is one of constant learning, understanding, and adaptation, driven by a shared commitment to safeguarding their organisations and the diverse communities they serve.

Asia

The diverse continent of Asia presents a fascinating challenge for creating and implementing security-conscious organisations. With an array of cultural values, political systems, and levels of technological adoption, the strategies deployed must be as adaptable and resilient as the continent itself.

In Asia, respect for hierarchy and collectivism often precede business practices and decision-making processes. To weave security consciousness into the fabric of organisations here, one must understand and respect these cultural nuances. This understanding can empower leaders to tailor their approaches, ensuring they resonate with their teams and promote a unified front against cyber threats.

The rapid technological growth observed in many Asian countries further complicates the landscape. With advancements in digital capabilities, organisations must be vigilant against a dual threat: the allure of cutting-edge technologies and the vulnerabilities they may introduce. Here, the balance between harnessing the power of technology and mitigating its risks becomes crucial.

Moreover, engaging employees in a manner that resonates culturally will enhance embedding security practices. From educational initiatives to the integration of behavioural science, these efforts must align with local values and beliefs to effectively foster a security-minded ethos. The goal is to move beyond compliance, cultivating a mindset where security becomes second nature to every individual.

Finally, continuous adaptation and improvement are key. Asia's landscape is not static, nor should the strategies to protect its organisations. Leaders must remain agile, ready to evolve their approaches to new threats and opportunities. This dynamic stance on security ensures that organisations not only withstand the challenges of today but are also primed to counter future threats with confidence and resilience.

Therefore, embracing the uniqueness of Asia's cultural and technological landscape lies at the heart of creating a security-conscious organisation. It's not merely about implementing policies but fostering an environment where security is ingrained in the collective consciousness - driving a more robust and resilient response to the modern world's cyber threats.

Latin America

In addressing the pursuit of enhanced cyber resilience, an exploration into the Latin American landscape reveals a tapestry of cultural, socio-economic, and political factors that uniquely shape its security posture. This region, characterised by its vibrant cultures and rapidly evolving technological landscapes, presents opportunities and challenges for creating a security-conscious organisation. To forge a path towards greater resilience, leaders must grasp the nuanced interplay between these elements and their impact on security strategies.

Understanding the cultural perspective in Latin America can't be overstated. The region's historical emphasis on communal values and interpersonal relationships plays a pivotal role in adopting and enforcing security protocols. Leveraging these cultural traits to foster a collaborative security culture can significantly enhance the effectiveness of organisational security measures. It encourages a collective responsibility among employees to safeguard not just their assets but also the integrity of their community.

In the realm of technological advancement, Latin America is on a trajectory marked by rapid digitisation and widespread adoption of mobile technology. This digital leap forward, while a boon for economic growth and connectivity, introduces a myriad of security vulnerabilities. Therefore, organisations operating in this region must be agile, adapting their security frameworks to counter emerging cyber threats without stifling innovation. Integrating technological solutions that respect cultural mores and promote user-friendly security practices will be key in achieving this balance.

Leadership in security culture within Latin American organisations requires a blend of authoritative knowledge and empathetic communication. Leaders must be champions of security, exemplifying and promulgating the behaviours and mindsets necessary to foster a resilient organisational culture. Training programmes tailored to the region's linguistic and cultural context will enhance the absorption and application of security principles, turning abstract concepts into relatable practices.

Moreover, Latin America's socio-economic diversity necessitates a flexible approach to security strategy formulation. Strategies should be scalable and adaptable to fit the varied needs of organisations operating in different countries within the region. This includes recognising disparities in technical infrastructure and regulatory environments and designing security initiatives that are both inclusive and effective.

Ultimately, the journey towards a secure and resilient organisation in Latin America hinges on the ability to interweave technological solutions with a deep understanding of cultural dynamics. By embracing rich diversity and leveraging communal values for collective security, leaders can navigate the complexities of the digital age. Through education, technological empowerment, and leadership, a truly security-conscious culture will emerge - capable of withstanding the cyber threats of today and tomorrow.

Africa

Within the scope of creating a security-conscious organisation, Africa presents both unique challenges and promising opportunities. The continent's diverse cultural landscape and dynamic economic environment necessitate a tailored approach to cultivating resilience against cyber threats. This sub-section aims to guide leaders in understanding and navigating the intricacies of African contexts in fostering a robust security culture.

As we delve into Africa's participation in the global discourse on security, it's evident that traditional security measures alone are no longer sufficient. The digital era has ushered in sophisticated threats that require equally sophisticated responses. With its rapid technological adoption, the African market stands at the precipice of substantial digital transformation but is also vulnerable to the security risks accompanying technological advancements.

To address these needs, looking beyond technical solutions and fostering a security culture deeply embedded in the organisation's ethos is imperative. This culture must reflect the African context, wherein communal values and collective responsibility play significant roles. A security-conscious culture in this context leverages these communal values, turning them into a strategic advantage. It involves creating awareness and understanding across all levels of the organisation, ensuring that security is not just the domain of the IT department but a shared responsibility.

Leadership within African organisations must champion security culture by example, demonstrating a commitment to secure practices in every action. This leadership influences the organisational attitude towards security, setting the tone for a culture that values vigilance and responsibility. Training leaders for security awareness is about imparting knowledge and inspiring a transformation that cascades from the top down.

Engagement strategies in Africa must also be localised and contextual, recognising the nuances of different cultures. This might include utilising local languages in security training materials or aligning security initiatives with local values and social norms. Such localisation ensures that security measures are not seen as foreign impositions but as relevant and essential to the well-being of the community and the organisation.

Finally, leveraging technology in Africa means acknowledging the digital divide and working within existing frameworks to ensure inclusivity. Technological security solutions must be accessible and practical, considering the varying levels of technology penetration across regions. It's about integrating technological solutions with cultural initiatives, where technology is an enabler for a security-conscious culture rather than a standalone answer.

Middle East

Within the richly diverse tapestry of global business, the Middle East stands out as a uniquely complex and dynamically evolving region, especially regarding security. For leaders aiming to foster a security-conscious organisation in this part of the world, understanding the Middle Eastern cultural and socio-political context is essential. With its blend of ancient traditions and rapid modernisation, this region requires a nuanced approach to developing and implementing effective security strategies that respect cultural values.

The Middle East's geopolitical landscape, marked by its strategic economic importance and political intricacies, profoundly impacts security considerations. The regional focus on industries such as oil and gas, finance, and telecommunications increases the necessity for robust cybersecurity measures to protect assets from increasingly sophisticated cyber threats.

Moreover, the Middle East's social and cultural dimensions, including a strong emphasis on trust and personal relationships, play a pivotal role in shaping security practices. Leaders need to realise that in this context, security measures can't just be imposed; they need to be woven into the fabric of organisational culture. Therefore, strategies for mindset change must be tailored to respect and integrate local customs and values, making engagement with employees a critical component of success.

Leadership in security culture within the Middle Eastern context means navigating a landscape where respect for authority figures is paramount. Thus, training leaders for security awareness goes beyond mere knowledge transfer - it's about instilling the values of responsibility, vigilance, and community welfare in every decision and action. Leaders must exemplify the security culture they wish to cultivate, demonstrating a commitment that inspires others to follow suit.

In addition, the technological landscape in the Middle East, with its rapid adoption of digital innovations, offers both opportunities and challenges for security. Integrating technological solutions with cultural initiatives must be done thoughtfully, ensuring that technologies are not just imposed but adopted in ways congruent with societal norms and values.

This approach enhances security and builds a sense of ownership and responsibility among stakeholders at all levels.

Creating a security-conscious organisation in the Middle East involves acknowledging the unique blend of challenges and opportunities this vibrant region presents. Embracing cultural diversity, leading by example, and thoughtfully leveraging technology can help organisations not only protect against threats but also become more resilient and adaptable to the evolving security landscape.

Thus, for leaders working in or with the Middle East, the journey towards enhanced security is not just about implementing strategies - it's about forging pathways that respect and reflect the region's rich cultural heritage and values. This approach fosters a resilient security culture and contributes to building trust and collaboration, which are essential for success in today's interconnected world.

Australia

Increasingly at the forefront of embedding a robust security culture within its organisations, Australia demonstrates a proactive approach in crafting environments resilient to cyber threats. In this landscape, Australian businesses, IT, and security leaders are pivotal in driving the change needed to fortify against the burgeoning spectrum of security risks. The Australian case presents an instructive blueprint on how a synergy between technological innovation and cultural transformation can significantly augment an organisation's security posture.

The Australian government's active engagement in cybersecurity initiatives provides a conducive backdrop for businesses to thrive securely. The emphasis on comprehensive cybersecurity strategies and the implementation of the Australian Cyber Security Centre (ACSC) guidelines underscore the national priority accorded to cybersecurity. This governmental support is a crucial enabler for organisations, facilitating the establishment of a security-conscious culture through policy and practice.

Australia's approach to building a resilient security culture is multifaceted in the corporate realm. It involves a solid commitment to education and continuous learning, recognising that the human element is as critical as the technological defences. Australian organisations increasingly invest in training programmes to enhance staff awareness and understanding of cyber risks. Such initiatives are not merely about disseminating information but are aimed at fostering a mindset where every employee feels responsible for the organisation's security.

Moreover, Australian businesses demonstrate a commendable integration of technology with cultural change initiatives. By leveraging advanced security technologies, such as AI and machine learning for threat detection and response, coupled with a strong organisational culture that values security, they create a resilient defence against cyber threats. Adopting best practices in technology deployment, focusing on user-friendliness and integration into daily workflows, ensures that security enhancements are not a hindrance but an enabler of business processes.

The success of Australia's approach also lies in its leadership's ability to drive cultural change. Leaders within Australian organisations are not merely advocates of security; they embody the principles of a security-conscious culture. Leaders inspire their teams to adopt and uphold secure practices by setting examples through their actions and decisions. This leadership commitment imbues security into the fabric of organisational culture, making it a shared value rather than an imposed requirement.

To emulate Australia's success in building resilient security cultures, leaders worldwide must recognise the importance of a holistic approach. This includes integrating technological solutions with strong cultural practices, empowering employees through education, and exemplifying secure practices by leadership. Australia's journey underscores the message that fostering a security-conscious culture is beneficial and essential in combatting cyber threats. The strides made by Australian organisations offer valuable lessons and inspiration for creating more secure environments in the face of evolving global cyber challenges.

In summary, security strategies cannot be one-size-fits-all; they must be tailored to the specific cultural contexts in which they are implemented. Geographic culture influences various aspects of behaviour, communication, and decision-making processes, all of which are crucial for the success of security initiatives. By understanding the local culture, organisations can anticipate potential challenges and design strategies that resonate with the local population.

Chapter 7

Psychological Safety

Fostering a culture where cybersecurity practices are adhered to, understood, and respected by all employees requires more than just enforcing strict rules or conducting routine training sessions. It necessitates creating a safe working environment where employees feel empowered to learn, grow, and make mistakes as part of developing cybersecurity awareness and practices.

Creating a Culture of Psychological Safety

Psychological safety has gained significant attention in recent years, particularly within organisational behaviour and learning. It refers to an environment where individuals feel secure enough to take interpersonal risks, such as admitting a mistake or asking for help, without fear of embarrassment, retribution, or other negative consequences. In the realm of cybersecurity, psychological safety becomes even more crucial.

A cyber psychological safety policy, sanctioned by the highest levels of leadership, is essential in fostering this environment. When employees know they can report cybersecurity mistakes - such as accidentally clicking on a phishing link or misconfiguring a security setting - without fear of punishment, they are more likely to come forward, allowing the organisation to promptly and effectively address issues. This transparency helps prevent minor errors from escalating into significant breaches and ensures the team learns from individual mistakes.

The Role of Leadership in Building Trust

Trust between employees and leadership is the cornerstone of a mature cybersecurity culture. When senior leaders visibly support and participate in cybersecurity initiatives, they send a powerful message that cybersecurity is a shared responsibility and that leaders are committed to creating an environment where employees can engage openly with cybersecurity practices without the fear of punitive repercussions.

A *cyber psychological safety policy* must be explicitly endorsed by the organisation's senior leadership, such as the CEO and the board of directors. This endorsement should be communicated clearly and frequently, emphasising that the organisation values learning from mistakes over blaming individuals for errors. Such a policy should outline the procedures for reporting and addressing cybersecurity incidents and the principles of trust, support, and continuous learning underpinning it.

The Benefits of a Trust-Based Approach

When employees trust that their organisation values their contributions and supports their learning, they are more likely to engage proactively with cybersecurity training and best practices. They become partners in the organisation's security efforts rather than mere followers of the rules. This proactive engagement can lead to several positive outcomes, including:

Increased Reporting of Incidents: Employees are more likely to report suspicious activities or their own mistakes if they trust that doing so will not lead to negative consequences. This early reporting is crucial in preventing minor issues from becoming major security breaches.

Enhanced Learning and Improvement: When mistakes are reported and analysed without blame, the organisation can use these incidents as learning opportunities. This collective learning helps improve security practices across the board, as the organisation can refine its policies and training based on real-world experiences.

More robust Security Culture: Trust fosters a culture where cybersecurity is seen as a collective responsibility. Employees feel a sense of ownership and pride in protecting their organisation's digital assets, leading to more vigilant and responsible behaviour.

Resilience in the Face of Threats: A trust-based culture equips the organisation to respond more effectively to security incidents. When employees are engaged and informed, they can act swiftly and confidently, helping mitigate potential threats' impact.

Implementing a Cyber Psychological Safety Policy

To successfully implement a cyber psychological safety policy, the following steps should be considered:

1. **Leadership Endorsement:** Secure visible and vocal support from the organisation's senior leaders. This endorsement should be part of all major communications and cybersecurity initiatives.

2. **Clear Policy Communication:** Develop a comprehensive policy document that outlines the principles of psychological safety in the context of cybersecurity. This document should be easily accessible and regularly referenced in training and meetings.

3. **Regular Training and Reinforcement:** Incorporate the policy's principles into regular cybersecurity training. Use real-world examples to demonstrate how the policy benefits individuals and the organisation.

4. **Open Channels for Feedback:** Establish transparent and anonymous channels for employees to report mistakes, suggest improvements, and ask questions about cybersecurity practices. Ensure that these channels are well-publicised and accessible.

5. **Celebrate Learning from Mistakes:** Publicly acknowledge instances where a mistake was reported and led to improvements in security practices. This reinforces the value of transparency and learning within the organisation.

Creating a safe working environment where employees feel comfortable making mistakes is not just a nice to have but a crucial component of a robust cybersecurity strategy. Organisations can build the trust necessary to encourage proactive engagement with cybersecurity practices by implementing a cyber psychological safety policy endorsed by senior leadership. This trust is the foundation upon which meaningful and lasting change in cybersecurity behaviours can be achieved, ultimately leading to a more resilient and secure organisation.

Chapter 8

Security Champions

In enhancing organisational resilience to cyber threats, the role of Security Champions cannot be overstated. Security Champions are the vital link between the broader security team and other departments, fostering a culture where security is everyone's responsibility. By embedding individuals with specialised security knowledge within various teams, organisations can significantly amplify their defence mechanisms against cyber threats. These champions are not just advisors but also role models who advocate for best practices and ensure their teams have the knowledge to identify and mitigate risks. They serve as the eyes and ears on the ground, providing essential feedback to security teams about potential vulnerabilities and the effectiveness of current security measures.

Identifying and selecting the right individuals to become Security Champions is a critical step towards bolstering an organisation's security posture. Ideal candidates exhibit a keen interest in cybersecurity, regardless of their formal role within the company. They can bridge the gap between technical and non-technical staff, making security more accessible and understandable. The selection process should emphasise technical acumen and soft skills like communication and leadership, as these champions will need to advocate for security practices and influence their colleagues positively. Organisations should strive to identify potential champions across different departments to ensure a wide-reaching and inclusive approach to security.

Once selected, providing tailored training and resources is paramount. Their training should cover the technical aspects of cybersecurity and the soft skills required to communicate and lead within their teams effectively. It's about empowering them with the knowledge and tools they need to act proactively against threats and to foster a security-minded culture within their domains. Creating strategies for champion engagement - such as regular meet-ups, forums for sharing best practices, and ongoing learning opportunities - can keep the champions motivated and up-to-date with the latest cybersecurity trends and tactics. Ultimately, the success of a Security Champion program hinges on continuous support and recognition from leadership, underscoring the program's value to the organisation's overall security strategy.

The Role and Importance of Security Champions

In an era of prevalent and continuously evolving cyber threats, the importance of fostering a robust security culture within an organisation cannot be overstated. Within this framework, the role of Security Champions emerges as both critical and transformative. These individuals operate as the vital link between the broader IT security team and the rest of the company, embodying the front line of defence in the battle against cyber threats.

Security Champions serve a pivotal function in extending the reach of the security team into departments that might not otherwise engage deeply with cybersecurity practices. By embedding these champions within various teams, organisations can ensure that security becomes a shared responsibility rather than being viewed as a domain exclusive to the IT security department. This approach demystifies security issues and integrates them into the company's daily operations and culture.

The importance of Security Champions goes beyond mere advocacy for best practices. These individuals are instrumental in identifying and addressing security vulnerabilities within their respective departments. Their unique position enables them to understand the specific challenges and nuances of their teams, making them adept at tailoring security recommendations that are both effective and practicable.

Furthermore, they play a crucial role in education and awareness. They provide a relatable point of contact for employees with questions or concerns about security issues. By offering guidance and training tailored to their teams' context, the champions help build a more knowledgeable workforce that can recognise and respond to security threats.

The motivational aspect of having Security Champions cannot be ignored. Their enthusiasm and commitment to security can inspire others to adopt a more proactive stance towards cybersecurity. This influence is critical in creating a culture where security is valued and prioritised by everyone, not just the security professionals.

In addition to fostering a security culture, champions are essential in implementing security policies. They ensure that these policies are not only adhered to but also adapted to fit the operational realities of their teams. This adaptability ensures that security measures are effective and aligned with business objectives, avoiding the common pitfall of viewing security as a hindrance to productivity.

The strategic importance of Security Champions extends to incident response and crisis management. Champions can be the initial point of contact in a security breach, facilitating rapid communication and response within their teams. Their intimate knowledge of their department's operations provides invaluable insights while resolving security incidents and minimising disruption and damage.

From a leadership perspective, the role of Security Champions is also significant in driving change within the organisation. They act as role models, demonstrating the importance of security in their actions and decision-making processes. This leadership by example is decisive in instilling a security-first mindset across all levels of the organisation.

Crucially, implementing the program signals an organisation's commitment to security at the highest levels. This commitment is reassuring to employees and builds trust with customers, partners, and regulators. In today's environment, where data breaches can severely damage reputations and bottom lines, such trust is invaluable.

Moreover, Security Champions facilitate continuous improvement in security practices. By being closely involved in their teams' day-to-day operations, they can provide timely feedback on what works and what does not, feeding into a cycle of constant iteration and enhancement of security measures.

The selection and training of the champions are also key to their effectiveness. Organisations must adopt a strategic approach to identifying individuals with the requisite technical knowledge and soft skills necessary to communicate and influence their colleagues effectively. Tailored training programs can equip these champions with the tools to succeed in their roles, ensuring they remain up-to-date with the latest security trends and best practices.

Ultimately, the role is about more than improving security; it's about changing an organisation's very culture. By embedding security within the company's DNA, champions help create an environment where security is not seen as a cost or an inconvenience but as a critical component of success and resilience.

In summary, the role and importance of Security Champions within an organisation must be considered. They are the linchpins in creating a security-conscious culture, ensuring that security practices evolve to meet changing threats and embedding a sense of shared responsibility for cybersecurity across all employees. As organisations navigate the complex landscape of cyber threats, the role of Security Champions will only grow in significance, making their support and development a key priority for leaders.

Identifying and Selecting Security Champions

As we've laid the groundwork for understanding the evolving landscape of security threats and the vital role of culture in bolstering an organisation's security posture, we arrive at a pivotal component of crafting a resilient security culture: the identification and selection of Security Champions. This section will guide you through pinpointing and enlisting these critical allies within their organisations.

It's not merely about assigning a new title or role within your team. It's about recognising and empowering individuals naturally inclined towards security practices and with the enthusiasm to spearhead security initiatives. These champions act as vital links between the security team and the rest of the organisation, embodying and promoting a culture of security awareness and best practices.

Identifying potential champions requires a thoughtful approach. Look for individuals keen on security matters, even if their primary role isn't security-centric. These people consistently advocate for strong passwords, are cautious about phishing attempts, and express interest in cybersecurity news and trends. Their passion for security and day-to-day work positions them to influence their peers positively.

Selection criteria should go beyond mere enthusiasm, however. A good Security Champion exhibits strong communication skills, is willing to learn, and demonstrates problem-solving abilities. They should be respected within their teams, capable of motivating others, and show initiative in tackling security-related challenges. It's also beneficial if they understand the organisation's workflows and processes, as this knowledge enables them to identify and address security vulnerabilities effectively.

Engagement with potential champions is crucial. Start with informal conversations to gauge their interest and willingness to take on the role. Discuss the expectations and responsibilities associated with being a Security Champion, ensuring they understand the commitment and the impact they can make. Emphasise the support and resources they will receive, highlighting how this role offers personal and professional development opportunities.

Training and resources are a cornerstone of empowering your Security Champions and preparing them to carry out their roles effectively. This aspect is so critical that it merits its dedicated discussion. Still, at this stage, it's essential to acknowledge that selected champions need ongoing support to develop the expertise required to advocate for and implement security best practices within their teams.

Recognition and reward mechanisms should be established to acknowledge the efforts and contributions of the champions. This not only motivates the champions but also raises the profile of security culture within the organisation. Celebrating successes and learning from challenges should be a shared journey, reinforcing the collective responsibility for security.

Integration into security planning and decision-making processes is essential. They should not operate in silos but rather be included in discussions on security policies, procedures, and strategies. This inclusion provides them with a broader perspective. It ensures that the voices of different parts of the organisation are heard in security conversations, leading to more practical and inclusive security practices.

Establishing a community of practice among champions fosters collaboration and knowledge sharing. Regular meetings, workshops, and forums where champions can share experiences, challenges, and solutions will strengthen their capability to serve effectively in their roles. This community should be dynamic, continuously evolving to address new security challenges and incorporate fresh perspectives.

To create a successful Security Champions program, leadership buy-in is non-negotiable. Leaders must endorse the program, provide the necessary resources, and often participate in the process themselves. Their active support not only legitimises the program but also underscores the centrality of security to the organisation's mission and values.

Diversity within the group is critical. Ensuring that champions represent various departments, roles, and backgrounds enriches the program, bringing insights and experiences to bear on security challenges. This diversity reflects the organisation and helps ensure that security initiatives are relevant and accessible to everyone.

Feedback from the champions on the program's effectiveness must be encouraged and acted upon. This feedback loop is vital for continuous improvement, allowing the organisation to adjust training, support, and the overall approach to maximising the impact of its champions.

The role of Security Champions is ongoing, adapting to evolving threats and changing organisational landscapes. Identifying and selecting these champions is not a one-time task but a continuous effort. Organisations must remain vigilant and look for potential champions who can contribute fresh energy and ideas to the program.

In summary, Security Champions are pivotal in building a resilient security culture. Identifying and selecting the right individuals for this role demands a strategic approach, centred around passion for security, capability to influence, and a commitment to fostering a secure environment. Through thoughtful engagement, comprehensive training, and unwavering support, Security Champions can catalyse a transformative security culture within any organisation.

As we delve further into the roles, training, and strategies for engaging Security Champions, remember that their success hinges on continuous support and recognition from all levels of the organisation. Together, champions and leadership can forge a path towards a more secure, aware, and resilient organisation, ready to face the challenges of a rapidly evolving security landscape.

Training and Resources for Security Champions

Implementing Security Champions within an organisation marks a pivotal step towards enhancing its security posture. However, selecting appropriate individuals for this role is merely the beginning. Equipping these champions with the necessary training and resources is fundamental to their success and, by extension, the organisation's resilience to cyber threats. This section will delve into the types of training and resources essential for Security Champions, providing a roadmap for leaders to follow.

First and foremost, Security Champions must comprehensively understand the current cyber threat landscape. This includes but isn't limited to, knowledge of how these threats evolve and the tactics employed by adversaries to breach organisational defences. A foundational course covering these aspects and updates on emerging threats should be a cornerstone of their ongoing education.

Beyond the foundational courses, technical training tailored to the organisation's specific IT environment is indispensable. The champions should know the technology stack used within their teams and the associated security best practices. This may involve hands-on training with the security tools in place, from intrusion detection systems to vulnerability management software.

Equally important is the development of soft skills. Security Champions often serve as a bridge between the IT/security team and the wider organisation. Thus, training in communication, influencing, and negotiation skills is vital. They need to be adept at conveying the importance of security measures in a manner that engages and motivates their colleagues.

Scenario-based training exercises are an excellent way to instill practical know-how. They can simulate real-world cyber incidents, challenging Security Champions to apply their technical knowledge and problem-solving skills in a high-pressure environment. The learnings derived from these exercises are invaluable, fostering a proactive security culture.

Access to a repository of resources is equally critical. This may encompass security policies, guidelines, checklists, and templates that

Champions can refer to and disseminate within their teams. An internal or external knowledge base, updated with the latest security research, white papers, and case studies, can be a dynamic learning tool.

Networking opportunities with security professionals outside the organisation can provide fresh perspectives and insights. Encouraging security champions to participate in security forums, conferences, and webinars not only aids their professional development but also benefits the organisation by keeping them abreast of industry trends and practices.

It's also beneficial to foster a constructive relationship between the champions and the IT and security departments. Regular meetings to discuss new threats, incidents, and security strategies can foster a culture of transparency and collaboration. This ensures that Security Champions are not operating in silos but are integrated into the broader security ecosystem of the organisation.

The provision of certifications and recognitions can be a further incentive. Achieving accredited certifications not only validates their expertise but also elevates their status within the organisation, making security a more integral part of the organisational culture.

Practical tools are a must. These include access to security software, vulnerability scanners, and other technologies enabling them to identify and address security issues within their teams proactively. Equipping them with these tools demonstrates the organisation's commitment to security and empowers champions to take definitive action.

Feedback mechanisms should be established to ensure that training and resources remain relevant and practical. Security Champions should have a forum to provide input on the training programmes and available resources, offering insights based on their experiences on the front lines.

The focus should be on continuous learning. Cyber threats are continuously evolving, and so should the knowledge and skills of those guarding against them. An annual or bi-annual review of the training curriculum and resources is advisable to keep pace with the advances in cyber threats and security technologies.

It's imperative that the training and resources provided are digestible and accessible. Consideration should be given to the varying levels of prior knowledge among Security Champions, with content tailored to meet these differing needs. An overly technical or complex programme can be off-putting to those without a deep IT background, potentially hindering their engagement.

Finally, an ethos of shared learning and collaboration among the team can amplify the impact of any training programme. Facilitating platforms for champions to share experiences, solutions, and best practices cultivates a vibrant and engaged security community within the organisation. This, in turn, enhances the organisation's collective security intelligence and resilience.

In summary, the training and resources provided to Security Champions are critical to their effectiveness and the organisation's overall security posture. A well-considered, dynamic programme encompassing technical and soft skills, continuous learning, and community building lays the foundation for a robust, resilient security culture. As leaders, it's your prerogative to ensure that security champions are empowered with the knowledge, skills, and tools they need to take charge of safeguarding your organisation against cyber threats.

Strategies for Champion Engagement

The identification and selection of the champions are crucial, yet the journey towards transforming them into influential catalysts for security awareness doesn't end there. It's essential to effectively engage these champions, ensuring they remain motivated, informed, and influential within their respective domains.

One effective strategy is to provide champions with a platform to share insights and experiences. Regular meetings or forums where champions can exchange knowledge, discuss challenges, and brainstorm solutions are critical in keeping them engaged. Such interactions empower them and strengthen the community, enhancing their ability to drive cultural change.

Training is another cornerstone of engagement. Offering continuous learning opportunities beyond initial training sessions is vital. Advanced workshops on the latest cybersecurity threats, defense mechanisms, and resilience strategies will ensure that champions remain at the forefront of security knowledge. Their role is dynamic; as threats evolve, so too must their expertise.

Acknowledgement is vital to sustaining motivation among Security Champions. Recognising and celebrating their contributions, big or small, boosts morale and encourages a persistent security-first mindset. Public recognition, awards, or even simple gestures of appreciation can make a significant difference.

Empowering champions with autonomy in promoting security within their teams can lead to innovative approaches to awareness and training. Encouraging creativity in their engagement methods can uncover uniquely impactful strategies tailored to specific team dynamics and cultures.

Equipping champions with the right tools and resources is imperative. Access to up-to-date information, educational materials, and security tools enables them to perform their roles effectively and more compellingly engage with their colleagues.

Creating a sense of ownership among Security Champions helps instil a personal commitment to the security agenda. When Champions feel responsible for their area's security posture, they're more likely to take proactive steps and go the extra mile to foster a security-conscious environment.

Setting clear and achievable goals for Security Champions helps them track progress and maintain their focus on key priorities. These goals should be aligned with the organisation's overall security strategy and tailored to their specific roles and capabilities.

Feedback loops between champions, their peers, and senior leadership are critical. Encouraging open dialogue about what's working and what isn't helps refine strategies and approaches, ensuring champions' efforts are as effective as possible.

Peer mentoring within the network can facilitate knowledge sharing and support among newer and more experienced champions. This accelerates the learning curve for incoming champions and fosters a supportive community that values continuous improvement.

Involving champions in security policy development can also give them a sense of ownership and investment in the organisation's security culture. This involvement also ensures that policies are practical, understandable, and more likely to be embraced by the broader employee base.

Champion-led initiatives like security awareness weeks or hackathons can stimulate organisational engagement and learning. These events allow them to showcase their leadership and organisational skills while emphasising the importance of security in a practical, hands-on way.

Fostering collaboration between the champions and other organisational initiatives, such as wellness programs or diversity and inclusion efforts, can broaden the perspective and reach of the security culture. Integrating security awareness into various aspects of organisational life makes it more relatable and ingrained in the everyday.

Finally, measuring the impact of Security Champions on the organisation's security posture is critical. By quantifying their influence, you can justify the investment in the program and identify areas for further improvement and scaling.

In summary, engaging Security Champions effectively requires a multifaceted approach, combining training, support, recognition, and continuous improvement. By adopting these strategies, you can ensure the champions are well-prepared and deeply motivated to spearhead a cultural shift towards enhanced security awareness across the organisation.

Chapter 9

Future-Proofing Security

In the relentless chase to stay ahead of emerging cyber threats, the key to not just surviving but thriving in tomorrow's security landscape lies in crafting security strategies that are both scalable and adaptable. As we delve into the essence of future-proofing security, we must anticipate future threats with a forward-thinking mindset. This strategic foresight isn't about predicting the future with pinpoint accuracy but about preparing to respond flexibly to various possible security scenarios.

The cultivation of such resilience hinges on a foundation of continuous learning, where knowledge of evolving threats is disseminated promptly throughout the organisation. Furthermore, embracing scalable and adaptable security strategies means developing systems and processes that can adjust and expand in response to an ever-changing threat landscape. This approach empowers businesses, IT, and security leaders not merely to react to threats as they arise but to anticipate changes and proactively adapt defences. By prioritising adaptability and scalability in security planning, leaders can ensure that their organisations are prepared for today's threats and positioned to tackle tomorrow's challenges.

This chapter aims to serve as both a compass and a roadmap, guiding you through the essential principles of creating a security posture that is resilient to the unforeseeable twists and turns of the future.

Anticipating Future Threats

In the rapidly evolving realm of security, staying a step ahead isn't just a tactic; it's necessary to safeguard any organisation's future. Anticipating future threats requires a forward-thinking mindset that combines keen observation of technological trends with an understanding of human behaviour and organisational dynamics.

The landscape of security threats metamorphoses with each technological advance. Integrating increasingly sophisticated technologies into our daily operations inadvertently opens new doors for cyber threats to seep through. This constant state of flux demands that leaders remain vigilant and cultivate a culture of continuous learning and adaptation within their teams.

Digital transformation, while driving efficiency and innovation, simultaneously broadens the attack surface that malicious actors can exploit. The Internet of Things (IoT), Artificial Intelligence (AI), and Machine Learning (ML) are prime examples where the convergence of operational technology (OT) and information technology (IT) creates complex security challenges. Hence, understanding the intricacies of these technologies and their implications on security is pivotal.

However, technology alone isn't the harbinger of threats. The human element remains one of the most unpredictable factors in the security equation. As organisations strive to foster a security-conscious culture, it's imperative to address the psychological aspects of security, including cognitive biases and behaviour patterns that can either mitigate or exacerbate vulnerabilities.

The rise of sophisticated social engineering attacks highlights the need for comprehensive behavioural training that goes beyond traditional security awareness. Engaging employees in regular, interactive training sessions can build a resilient frontline defense. Moreover, creating a culture where security is everyone's responsibility empowers individuals to act as vigilant guardians of their digital realm.

Another critical aspect of anticipating future threats is regulatory compliance. As governments worldwide tighten data protection laws, compliance becomes a moving target. Organisations must adhere to current regulations and prepare for impending changes affecting how data is processed, stored, and protected.

Collaboration across industries and sectors plays a crucial role in threat anticipation. Sharing intelligence about emerging threats and response strategies can bolster collective defense mechanisms. This cooperative approach enhances the ability to preempt attacks and mitigate their impacts.

Adopting a proactive security posture is key in the face of constantly evolving threats. This involves regular assessments of security measures, penetration testing, and red teaming exercises to identify and address vulnerabilities before they can be exploited. It's a continuous cycle of assessing, adapting, and enhancing security protocols to stay ahead of threats.

Sustainability in security practices also demands scalability. Security measures must evolve as organisations grow to accommodate increased complexity and scale. Scalable security architectures allow for the seamless integration of new technologies and the fortification of defenses without cumbersome overhauls.

Cloud security emerges as a significant concern in anticipating future threats. With more organisations relying on cloud services for storage, processing, and operations, ensuring data integrity in the cloud is paramount. Understanding the shared responsibility model of cloud security and implementing strong access controls and encryption is fundamental.

The role of AI and automation in future-proofing security cannot be overstated. Leveraging AI for predictive threat intelligence and automated threat detection systems can significantly enhance an organisation's ability to anticipate and respond to attacks. However, it's also essential to recognise the potential of AI in the hands of adversaries, necessitating advanced defensive measures.

The integration of physical security into cyber security strategies is a trend that's gaining momentum. As the lines between physical and cyber worlds blur, securing physical assets against cyber-enabled attacks becomes integral to a comprehensive security posture. This holistic approach ensures that security measures are not siloed but interwoven across all facets of the organisation.

Lastly, fostering a culture of innovation within security teams encourages the exploration of novel solutions and unconventional approaches to tackling future threats. Encouraging creativity and out-of-the-box thinking can unearth new strategies that keep organisations one step ahead of malicious actors.

In summary, anticipating future threats requires a blend of technological acuity, psychological insight, regulatory foresight, and collaborative effort. By embedding these principles into the fabric of their security strategies, leaders can build resilient organisations in the face of current threats but also adaptable to the challenges of tomorrow.

Scalable and Adaptable Security Strategies

As we delve into the essence of future-proofing security, it's crucial to foreground the necessity of security strategies that aren't just robust but also scalable and adaptable. The dynamic nature of cyber threats demands frameworks that can evolve with emerging technologies and sophisticated threat vectors.

The concept of scalability in security implies a system's capacity to handle a growing amount of work or its potential to accommodate growth. For leaders, designing a scalable security strategy means ensuring that security measures can be amplified without compromising on efficiency or effectiveness. This is particularly significant in an age where digital transformation initiatives are at the forefront of business growth.

Adaptability, on the other hand, refers to the ability of a system to adjust itself efficiently and quickly to changed or changing conditions. With the rapid pace of technological advancements, an adaptable security strategy ensures that organisations can swiftly respond to new threats and vulnerabilities. This approach necessitates a forward-thinking mentality, fostering an environment where continuous learning and agility are ingrained in the organisational culture.

Organisations must undertake a comprehensive risk assessment process to establish a scalable and adaptable security strategy. This involves identifying potential security threats, evaluating their likelihood of occurrence, and assessing their potential impact on business operations. Understanding the risk landscape enables organisations to prioritise security efforts and allocate resources more effectively.

Another fundamental aspect is embedding security into an organisation's DNA. This means going beyond traditional security training and awareness programs to create a culture where employees feel responsible for cyber security. Leveraging behavioural science principles can aid in crafting interventions that modify security behaviours on an individual and organizational level.

Technological agility plays a pivotal role in scalable and adaptable security. This entails adopting the latest security technologies and ensuring that the security infrastructure can integrate new tools and systems with minimal disruption. It's about building a modular security architecture where components can be easily upgraded or replaced as required.

Data analytics and intelligence gathering are instrumental in predicting and mitigating future threats. By harnessing the power of big data and machine learning, organisations can gain insights into emerging trends in cybercrime, assisting in the proactive adjustment of security strategies.

Collaboration is key to scalability and adaptability. This includes internal collaboration between departments to ensure a unified approach to security and external collaboration with industry peers, law enforcement, and security experts to share knowledge and best practices.

Incident response plans must be flexible and regularly updated to reflect the evolving threat landscape. Organisations should conduct periodic drills and simulations to test the effectiveness of their response strategies, enabling adjustments based on real-world scenarios.

Regulatory compliance is a moving target with jurisdictions worldwide updating their data protection and privacy legislation. A scalable and adaptable security strategy must account for these changes, maintaining compliance without hindering operational agility.

Organisations should employ a layered security approach. This strategy utilises multiple defensive layers to protect information systems, ensuring that if one layer fails, others are in place to thwart an attack. Such an approach is inherently more flexible as layers can be added or removed in accordance with the threat environment.

Finally, the role of leadership cannot be overstated in driving the scalability and adaptability of security strategies. Leaders must champion security as a core value, instilling a mindset that embraces change and innovation. This leadership stance fosters a culture where security measures are viewed as enablers of business continuity and growth rather than mere IT requirements.

In conclusion, as leaders navigate the complexities of the modern threat landscape, the principles of scalability and adaptability must be at the heart of their security strategies. This approach prepares organisations to face current threats and equips them to anticipate and mitigate future challenges. Organisations can create resilient security frameworks that support long-term business objectives by fostering continuous improvement, leveraging technological agility, and prioritising collaborative efforts.

Empowering organisations to adapt their security measures in the face of evolving threats is not just about protecting assets; it's about ensuring business viability in an increasingly digital world. As we move forward, let this be the mantra that guides our efforts: adopt, adapt, and advance. Through scalable and adaptable security strategies, our journey towards a more secure future continues with confidence and clarity.

Chapter **10**

Integrating Culture Change into Strategy

In the quest to fortify an organisation against the myriad of cyber threats, integrating culture change into the security strategy emerges as a pivotal endeavour. It begins with a robust evaluation of the existing cultural landscape within the organisation, pinpointing how perceptions, beliefs, and behaviours impact security practices. This evaluation sheds light on the present state and identifies the cultural touchstones that can serve as levers for transformative change. The journey from recognising these levers to implementing a change that permeates the entire organisational culture is intricate, necessitating a thoughtful approach that respects the nuances of the organisation's identity while steering it towards a security-first mentality.

Understanding the barriers and facilitators within the organisation's cultural fabric plays a critical role in shaping a security strategy that is both effective and culturally aware. Barriers often manifest as resistance to change, a lack of security awareness, or even deeply ingrained beliefs undermining security measures. Conversely, facilitators might include a strong sense of communal responsibility, a high regard for organisational integrity, or an existing culture of innovation that can be leveraged to foster a more security-conscious mindset. By tailoring the security strategy to account for these cultural dimensions, leaders can ensure that security initiatives are accepted and embraced across the organisation. This process requires a blend of clear communication, compelling motivation, and continuous education, ensuring that security becomes a core component of the organisation's identity.

At the heart of integrating culture change into security strategy lies the principle of continuous iteration and feedback. The saying 'culture eats strategy for breakfast' rings especially true in the realm of security, where the most sophisticated strategies can be rendered ineffective if they don't resonate with the cultural ethos of the organisation. Hence, incorporating behavioural insights to shape security behaviours and robust techniques for monitoring cultural change form the backbone of a responsive security strategy. Establishing feedback loops enables the ongoing refinement of security measures, ensuring they evolve with the cultural landscape and emerging cyber threats. This iterative process, grounded in a deep understanding of the organisation's culture and behavioural dynamics, empowers leaders to forge a resilient, security-conscious organisation poised to withstand future cyber challenges.

Evaluating the Current Cultural Landscape

As we delve into the realm of securing our organisations, it's imperative that we first take a step back to understand the cultural terrain that underpins our security strategies. The journey towards embedding an ironclad security culture within an organisation begins with a comprehensive evaluation of the existing cultural landscape. This section aims to guide leaders through the methods of assessing their current security culture, laying the foundational stone necessary for fostering a security-conscious organisation.

At the forefront of this evaluation is the deployment of surveys and questionnaires specifically designed to gauge employees' perceptions, attitudes, and behaviours toward security within the organisation. These tools can uncover invaluable insights into the workforce's awareness levels, their understanding of security policies, and their predisposition to adhere to security protocols. Not only do surveys provide a quantitative measure of the security culture, but they also open channels for employees to express concerns or suggest improvements.

Another critical methodology involves conducting interviews and focus groups. These qualitative approaches allow for deeper dives into the nuances of the organisational security culture. Through conversations with employees across various departments and levels of seniority, leaders can identify overt and subtle cultural influencers that impact security practices. Focus groups can unveil collective perceptions and shared experiences that surveys alone might not capture.

Beyond direct feedback mechanisms, observational studies serve as a powerful tool to evaluate the security culture. Observing employees in their natural working environment can assess their security behaviours versus what is reported in surveys or interviews. This method helps identify discrepancies between declared and real practices, revealing areas where the security culture may need strengthening.

Engaging in document analysis of existing security policies, training materials, and communication channels provides an understanding of the formal security culture as intended by the leadership. Reviewing these documents helps assess whether the security values espoused by the organisation align with the culture perceived and experienced by the employees. It also sheds light on potential communication or policy implementation gaps that could hinder building a robust security culture.

Utilising security incidents and near-miss data is another method to gauge the maturity of an organisation's security culture. Analysing patterns and root causes of security breaches or lapses can reveal weaknesses in the cultural fabric that allow such incidents to occur. This analysis not only aids in rectifying immediate vulnerabilities but also in understanding the organisational behaviours and attitudes that need to be shaped for improved security resilience.

Benchmarking against industry standards and peers offers a comparative view of an organisation's security culture. Understanding where one stands compared to others in the industry can highlight areas of strength and potential weaknesses. Moreover, it can serve as a motivational tool for organisations to strive towards best practices and excellence in security culture.

Integrating these various methods creates a comprehensive and multidimensional evaluation of an organisation's current security culture. However, this evaluation must be approached with an open mind and a willingness to listen and adapt. The findings from this assessment should not be viewed as a critique but rather as a stepping stone towards building a more secure and resilient organisation.

In light of these findings, it's essential to prioritise areas of improvement identified during the evaluation. Tackling these areas systematically can lead to significant enhancements in the security culture. This prioritisation must align with the organisation's security strategy to ensure coherence and effectiveness.

Communication of the evaluation findings with all stakeholders is paramount. Transparency in sharing the strengths and areas for improvement fosters a culture of trust and collaborative effort towards enhancing security practices. This communication must be clear, constructive, and aimed at galvanising collective action.

Setting benchmarks and goals based on the evaluation findings helps track progress towards a stronger security culture. These benchmarks must be realistic, measurable, and aligned with the organisation's overall objectives. Regular monitoring and reporting on these benchmarks instill a sense of accountability and motivates continuous improvement.

Engaging employees in evaluating and enhancing the security culture ensures their buy-in and active participation in security initiatives. Their firsthand experiences and insights are invaluable in crafting effective and practical measures to strengthen the security culture. Encouraging an open dialogue about security practices empowers employees to contribute positively to a secure organisational environment.

Finally, it's important to recognise that evaluating and enhancing the cultural landscape regarding security is an ongoing process. As external and internal factors evolve, so too will the security threats and challenges. The methods outlined here provide a framework for continually assessing and adapting the security culture, ensuring that the organisation remains resilient in the face of ever-changing cyber threats.

In summary, integrating culture change into your security strategy begins with thoroughly evaluating the current cultural landscape. By employing a mix of quantitative and qualitative methods, engaging with employees, and setting clear benchmarks and goals, organisations can lay the groundwork for a security-conscious culture. The journey requires commitment, adaptability, and collective effort, but the rewards - a robust and resilient security posture - are invaluable.

As we move forward in this book, we will delve deeper into the specifics of identifying cultural barriers and facilitators to security initiatives, principles of culturally aware security strategies, and techniques for monitoring cultural change. Each step is integral to building a security culture that protects the organisation and enhances its business operations and reputation.

Cultural Barriers and Facilitators

Identifying both the barriers and facilitators to security initiatives is crucial to bridging the gap between a current and a desired security culture within organisations. This step is about pinpointing issues and understanding the nuanced interplay between organisational culture and security protocols. We shall explore this interplay, offering insights into how leaders can navigate, leverage, and sometimes even reshape cultural elements to bolster their security posture.

At the outset, one must acknowledge that organisational cultures are as varied as the individuals that comprise them. Despite this diversity, certain commonalities exist which can either hinder or enhance security initiatives. A primary barrier often encountered is the perception of security measures as impediments to productivity or convenience. In fast-paced environments, security protocols can be seen as additional hurdles to navigate, leading to resistance or non-compliance from staff.

Moreover, an organisation's preexisting communication channels can either facilitate or obstruct the dissemination of security-related information. Hierarchical cultures with rigid communication protocols may slow the exchange of vital security alerts. In contrast, a more open, agile communication culture can prove beneficial in spreading awareness and fostering a security-conscious environment.

Another significant cultural barrier is the general level of security awareness among employees. In some cases, a lack of awareness or understanding can lead to a casual approach to security, where employees underestimate the importance of compliance with security policies. A misalignment between the perceived and actual risk levels among staff and management often compounds this.

However, it's not all hurdles. Some cultural elements can facilitate the implementation of robust security measures. A strong culture of trust within an organisation encourages open discussion about potential threats and vulnerabilities without fear of recrimination. This openness can lead to quicker identification of security gaps and a more proactive approach to addressing them.

Leadership commitment to security is another critical facilitator. When leaders exemplify and vocalise their commitment to security practices, it sets a tone for the whole organisation, encouraging a more security-conscious culture. This leadership role is not limited to directives but includes active participation in and endorsement of security training and awareness programs.

Furthermore, integrating security practices into everyday work routines can help overcome resistance to new security protocols. When security becomes a seamless aspect of organisational life, compliance is no longer seen as an additional task but as part of the normative behaviour expected within the organisation.

Encouraging employee involvement in developing and refining security initiatives can also be a potent facilitator. When employees are part of the conversation, they are more likely to understand the necessity of certain measures and, therefore, more inclined to adhere to them. This can also lead to innovative ideas on how to implement security measures to minimise disruption to workflows.

A thorough evaluation of the organisational culture is necessary to identify these barriers and facilitators. This can be achieved through surveys, interviews, and discussion forums that engage employees at all levels. Such evaluations should aim to uncover not just the explicit but also the tacit cultural norms governing organisational behaviour.

Once identified, the challenge lies in addressing these cultural barriers while capitalising on the facilitators. It requires a strategic approach that is sensitive to the organisation's unique cultural dynamics. Tailoring security initiatives to fit within these dynamics, rather than forcing change, is often more effective in achieving lasting improvements in security behaviour.

Integrating cultural awareness into the development of security strategies must be considered. It's not merely about implementing technical controls and protocols but about weaving security into the fabric of the organisational culture. This means moving beyond a compliance-focused approach to one that engages and motivates employees, making them active participants in securing the organisation.

To this end, the role of continuous education and reinforcement cannot be overstated. Cultivating a security-conscious culture is an ongoing process that requires regular updates, reminders, and training. Making security an integral part of onboarding and continuous professional development can help maintain high awareness and compliance levels.

Lastly, celebrating and recognising compliance with and contributions to security initiatives can act as a strong motivator for continued adherence. Recognition can come in various forms, from simple thank-you notes to awards for "Security Champions." Such recognition reinforces the importance of security within the organisation and helps build a positive association with security practices.

In summary, identifying cultural barriers and facilitators to security initiatives is a complex but essential component of integrating culture change into your security strategy. It requires a nuanced understanding of organisational culture and a strategic approach to embedding security within this culture. By navigating these barriers and leveraging facilitators, leaders can create a more resilient organisation that is better equipped to deal with the evolving landscape of cyber threats.

Principles of Culturally Aware Security Strategies

Integrating culturally aware security strategies within an organisation's security framework marks a critical juncture in the journey towards a more resilient security posture. In understanding that every culture perceives, interprets, and reacts to security threats differently, we embark on a mission to tailor security strategies that are effective and embraced across the board. At the heart of this endeavour lies a commitment to principles that respect and leverage cultural diversity, ensuring that security becomes a common thread weaving through the organisation's fabric.

First, empathy is at the core of culturally aware security strategies. Recognising the diverse backgrounds and perspectives of individuals within the organisation allows us to tailor communications and policies that resonate personally. This means going beyond the traditional one-size-fits-all approach to developing security protocols that acknowledge the uniqueness of each cultural group within the workforce.

Transparency is another pillar essential to cultivating trust and openness about security within an organisation. When security policies and practices are transparent, people are more likely to understand their importance and feel a sense of ownership over their contributions to the organisation's security. It encourages open dialogue about security concerns and fosters an environment where individuals feel comfortable sharing their perspectives and insights.

Engagement and participation must be actively encouraged to ensure that security is not seen as a top-down imposition but as a collective responsibility. Cultivating an atmosphere where everyone feels they have a stake in security empowers individuals to contribute their knowledge and skills. This participatory approach enhances the security culture and leverages diverse cultural insights to identify and mitigate risks effectively.

Adaptability in security strategies signifies the recognition that as cultures evolve, so too should the approaches to security. What works today might be less effective tomorrow, and strategy must be agile enough to adapt to emerging cultural and risk landscapes. This principle ensures that security practices remain relevant and aligned with organisational and cultural shifts.

Educational initiatives tailored to accommodate cultural nuances are crucial in raising awareness and understanding of security issues. By framing education and training in an engaging and relevant way to all cultural groups, organisations can improve the uptake of security practices and foster a more security-conscious workforce.

Leadership models that reflect and respect cultural diversity can significantly enhance the effectiveness of security strategies. Leaders who demonstrate cultural sensitivity and an understanding of different cultural norms and values can inspire trust and motivate their teams to adopt secure behaviours.

Culturally sensitive recognition and rewards systems can incentivise security-conscious behaviour in a manner that's meaningful to diverse groups within the organisation. Such systems encourage continued engagement with security practices by acknowledging and celebrating the contributions of all employees.

Integration of local knowledge and practices into the broader security strategy enriches the organisation's understanding and management of risks. Local employees can provide invaluable insights into cultural norms and behaviours that can influence the success of security measures. Leveraging this knowledge ensures that security practices are not only respectful of local customs but are also more likely to be adopted.

Multilingual resources and support ensure that security policies, protocols, and educational materials are accessible to everyone, regardless of their primary language. This inclusivity underscores the organisation's commitment to ensuring that all employees are informed, aware, and equipped to contribute to security efforts.

Collaboration across different departments and cultural groups fosters a holistic security approach. By breaking down silos and encouraging cross-functional teams to work together on security initiatives, organisations can create a more robust and comprehensive security posture that benefits from a diversity of perspectives and expertise.

In conclusion, the principles of culturally aware security strategies are designed to foster an inclusive environment where security is everyone's responsibility. By recognising and leveraging the strengths inherent in cultural diversity, organisations can build security frameworks that are more resilient to threats and more reflective of the global landscape in which they operate. These principles provide the foundation for a security-conscious culture that values, respects, and engages all members of the organisation, paving the way for a safer and more secure future.

Behavioural Insights to Shape Security Behaviours

The link between human behaviour and organisational security cannot be overstated. Behavioural insights offer a powerful lens through which we can understand and influence the actions individuals take in relation to security policies and practices. This section delineates the integration of behavioural insights into shaping security behaviours, pivotal for leaders aiming to foster a security-conscious organisation.

At the outset, it's imperative to acknowledge that security isn't solely a technical challenge but deeply intertwined with human psychology. People are the first line of defence and often, the weakest link. This duality makes it essential to delve into the cognitive biases, social influences, and decision-making processes that govern behaviour in the workplace.

Understanding the 'why' behind actions is the first step in influencing change. Behavioural insights draw on psychology to explain why individuals might bypass security protocols, such as the allure of convenience over compliance or the underestimation of cyber risks. Identifying these underlying factors enables the design of interventions that can nudge staff towards more secure behaviours.

One practical approach is to utilise the EAST framework, making actions **E**asy, **A**ttractive, **S**ocial, and **T**imely. For instance, simplifying security processes can address the barrier of perceived inconvenience, thus encouraging adherence. Similarly, highlighting the social norm of compliance within the organisation can leverage peer influence to promote secure behaviour.

Creating an environment that rewards secure behaviour is also crucial. Positive reinforcement can significantly bolster the adoption of desired security practices. Whether through recognition programs or tangible incentives, highlighting the value of secure behaviour can motivate employees beyond mere compliance.

Another key aspect is leveraging technology as an enabler rather than a barrier. Automated reminders for password changes or software updates, for instance, can lessen individuals' cognitive load, making security practices more adherent to human behaviour patterns.

Customising communication and training to resonate with diverse audiences within an organisation is also fundamental. A one-size-fits-all approach often falls flat. Tailored messages that consider the varied roles, responsibilities, and risk exposure can significantly improve engagement and uptake of secure behaviours.

Measuring the impact of behavioural interventions is vital for continuous improvement. Establishing metrics that quantify changes in behaviour, such as decreased incidents of phishing email clicks, provides tangible evidence of progress and areas needing further attention.

Pilot programmes are an excellent starting point to test the effectiveness of behavioural interventions before wider implementation. This iterative process allows for refining strategies based on real-world feedback and outcomes.

However, ethical considerations must be considered when utilising behavioural insights. Manipulation or coercion undermines trust and can negatively impact organisational culture. Transparency about the purposes and processes of behavioural interventions fosters trust and cooperation.

Empathy plays a central role in shaping security behaviours. Understanding the pressures and challenges employees face in their roles can guide the development of more compassionate and effective security solutions. Empathetic leadership can bridge the gap between policy mandates and practical, lived experience.

Embedding behavioural insights into security strategy isn't an instantaneous solution but a strategic, ongoing effort. It necessitates leadership commitment and a willingness to adapt based on evolving insights into human behaviour.

Successful integration of behavioural insights transforms security from a list of dos and don'ts into a shared value deeply ingrained in the organisational fabric. It cultivates a culture where secure behaviours are not just mandated but instinctive, creating a resilient organisation better equipped to face the cyber threats of tomorrow.

In summary, behavioural insights provide a critical tool in the arsenal of any organisation aiming to enhance its security posture. By understanding and shaping the human elements of security, businesses can achieve a synergy between people, processes, and technology, laying the foundation for a robust security culture that withstands the test of time.

Moving beyond traditional security training to a more nuanced understanding of human behaviour opens avenues for innovative, effective security strategies. This approach champions the human element as a strength to be leveraged rather than a vulnerability to be mitigated.

Measuring Cultural Improvements

Transitioning a business towards a security-conscious culture is an ongoing journey that requires continuous vigilance, assessment, and evolution. Monitoring cultural change and security enhancements is not merely about ticking boxes on a compliance checklist; it's about embedding a transformative process into the very fabric of an organisation. This section delves into effective techniques and strategies that facilitate this essential monitoring.

To begin with, it's imperative to establish clear, measurable objectives related to cultural change and security enhancements. These objectives might range from quantifiable targets like reducing phishing attack susceptibility to more qualitative goals such as improving employee engagement with security protocols.

Surveys and questionnaires are crucial tools for gauging the temperature of your organisation's culture. Regularly distributed, these tools can provide real-time insights into staff perceptions, attitudes, and knowledge surrounding security. However, crafting these instruments carefully is vital to elicit honest and constructive feedback.

Beyond surveys, focus groups can offer a deeper dive into the mindset of your workforce. By facilitating open discussions among diverse employee groups, organisations can uncover hidden concerns, suggestions, and misunderstandings that might not surface through more anonymous feedback channels.

Security audits and assessments are also key in measuring the tangible impacts of cultural shifts towards security. By periodically reviewing security practices, incident reports, and response times, businesses can evaluate the effectiveness of their cultural transformation efforts.

A complementary technique is the deployment of security metrics and benchmarks. These can range from the number of security incidents before and after culture change interventions, to metrics related to compliance with security practices, such as software updates and password changes. Tracking these over time paints a vivid picture of progress and areas for improvement.

Engagement metrics, particularly in the digital security training realm, can offer insights too. These might include completion rates for security training modules, engagement scores, or pre- and post-training assessment results. An uptick in these metrics can indicate a growing organisational commitment to security.

Another innovative approach is the utilisation of behavioural analytics. By analysing patterns in how employees interact with security systems and protocols, organisations can identify positive changes in behaviour that should be encouraged and risky behaviours that need to be addressed.

Peer reviews and internal discussion platforms can also foster an environment of continuous feedback. Encouraging employees to share their experiences and tips for adhering to security protocols can promote a culture of learning and mindfulness regarding security.

Implementing a recognition system for security-conscious behaviours is a technique for monitoring and actively promoting cultural change. Recognising and rewarding employees for proactive security can reinforce the desired culture shift and inspire others.

Security champions play a pivotal role in both monitoring and influencing cultural change. By liaising between the security team and the rest of the organisation, these champions can provide valuable on-the-ground insights on the evolving culture and effectiveness of security measures.

Lastly, integrating security metrics into broader business performance dashboards can ensure that security culture remains a central consideration in the organisation's overall strategy. This integration helps keep security at the forefront of business objectives and discussions.

Adopting an iterative approach to cultural change and security enhancements is crucial. The techniques outlined above should not be seen as one-off tasks but as components of a continuous improvement cycle. Organisations can foster a resilient and security-conscious culture by regularly revisiting objectives, updating strategies based on feedback, and innovating in response to emerging threats.

In summary, the journey towards an entrenched security culture is multifaceted and perpetual. Through diligent monitoring and adaptive strategies, organisations can protect against current threats and anticipate and mitigate future vulnerabilities. Fostering an environment that values security as an intrinsic part of its culture is the only way for businesses to thrive in the digital age truly.

In this transformative era, where security is not just a technical necessity but a cultural imperative, leaders are called upon to guide their organisations with vision, dedication, and an unwavering commitment to fostering a culture of security. It is this dedication to continuous improvement and cultural evolution that will define the resilient organisations of tomorrow.

Refine Strategies With Feedback Loops

In the dynamic world of cybersecurity, where threats evolve at an alarming pace, the importance of establishing robust feedback loops to refine security strategies cannot be overstated. It's paramount for leaders to recognise that the development of a security strategy is not a one-time task but an ongoing process that requires constant attention and adjustment.

Feedback loops stand as a critical mechanism for this iterative process, enabling organisations to adapt to new threats, understand the effectiveness of current security measures, and identify areas for improvement. By integrating feedback loops into their security approach, leaders can foster a culture of continual learning and resilience against cyber threats.

At the heart of an effective feedback loop is the collection of data and insights from various sources within the organisation. This includes insights from security systems, incident reports, employee feedback, and regular security assessments. The diverse nature of these sources ensures a comprehensive understanding of the security landscape and the effectiveness of implemented strategies.

Analysing this collected data is the next critical step. Organisations must have the capability to sift through this information to identify patterns, uncover weaknesses, and highlight successes. It's not just about finding what went wrong, but also about recognising what is working well, so these successes can be replicated and built upon.

Crucially, this analysis must then lead to action. Identified issues need to be addressed promptly, and strategies should be adjusted accordingly. This may involve updating policies, introducing new training programmes, or deploying new technologies. The ability to act swiftly on the insights gained from the feedback loop is what ultimately enhances an organisation's security posture.

For this process to be truly effective, it must engage stakeholders across the organisation. Security is not solely the domain of the IT department; it requires the involvement and cooperation of all employees. Therefore, feedback loops should incorporate contributions from a wide range of roles, ensuring that every perspective is considered and every voice has the opportunity to influence the security strategy.

Communication is a key element in this endeavour. The findings from the feedback loop analysis need to be shared across the organisation in a clear, understandable, and actionable manner. This not only helps to ensure that necessary changes are made but also serves to reinforce the value of everyone's input into the security process, thereby encouraging ongoing engagement and vigilance.

Furthermore, incorporating external feedback can provide additional insights that internal processes might miss. This can come from security partners, industry peers, and professional bodies. Their external viewpoint can shed light on emerging threats and trends that have yet to be experienced directly but need preparation and response strategies in place.

Establishing these feedback loops also serves as a foundation for developing a proactive rather than reactive security posture. By continuously monitoring and adjusting strategies based on feedback, organisations can anticipate potential security challenges and mitigate risks before they materialise into significant threats.

Technology plays a crucial role in enabling these feedback loops. Advanced analytics and AI-driven security tools can process vast amounts of data more efficiently than humanly possible, identifying anomalies and trends that might indicate new forms of attack or areas of vulnerability. However, technology alone is not the solution; it must be coupled with human insight and understanding to interpret data in the organisation's unique security landscape.

Establishing effective feedback loops requires a commitment to cultural change within the organisation. It's about creating an environment where security is seen as a collective responsibility and where continuous improvement is integral to the operational mindset. This cultural shift is crucial for effective feedback loops, as it encourages open dialogue, collaboration, and a shared commitment to security.

Moreover, the process of establishing and maintaining feedback loops should itself be subject to regular review. As organisations evolve and the security landscape changes, the mechanisms for feedback and how they are integrated into the security strategy may also need to adapt. This meta-loop ensures that the feedback process remains relevant and practical.

In summary, feedback loops are essential to an agile and resilient security strategy. They provide the mechanisms for continual assessment and adaptation, enabling organisations to respond effectively to evolving threats. By embedding these processes into the organisational culture, businesses can foster a proactive security posture that defends against threats and drives operational and strategic improvement.

The journey towards enhancing security is ongoing, and feedback loops are the navigational tools that guide organisations through the ever-changing threat landscape. By committing to these iterative processes, leaders can ensure that their security strategies are not static but evolve in line with the threats they face, ultimately achieving a more secure and resilient organisation.

Thus, taking the leap to integrate feedback loops into security strategies is not just about enhancing cybersecurity; it's about building a culture that values learning, adaptation, and collective responsibility for security. It's about making every individual in the organisation a proactive participant in safeguarding their digital and physical environments. This is the cornerstone of a security-conscious organisation, poised to meet today's and tomorrow's challenges with confidence and resilience.

Examples of Good Cyberculture Programmes

The benefits are profound when organisations foster a strong cybersecurity culture and encourage proactive behaviour. Unlike cyber incidents routinely published in the media, near-misses are commonly kept quiet for fear of impacting a business's brand. However, some real-world examples highlight the positive outcomes when cybersecurity is taken seriously.

NHS Digital (UK National Health Service) [13] [14]

NHS Digital plays a critical role in managing and securing the digital infrastructure of the UK's healthcare system. In the wake of the WannaCry ransomware attack in 2017, which severely impacted NHS services nationwide, NHS Digital embarked on a significant overhaul of its cybersecurity framework. The attack catalysed transformative changes within the organisation, particularly in how cybersecurity was perceived and managed.

NHS Digital implemented more rigorous security protocols, improved system patching practices, and enhanced incident response capabilities. A crucial element of their strategy was cultivating a strong cybersecurity culture among staff, which included regular training and awareness programs to reduce the risk of human error, a common vector in cyber-attacks.

---

[13] National Audit Office. (2018). *Investigation: WannaCry cyber attack and the NHS*. Retrieved from https://www.nao.org.uk/report/investigation-wannacry-cyber-attack-and-the-nhs/

[14] NHS Digital. (2018). *Lessons learned review of the WannaCry Ransomware Cyber Attack*. Retrieved from https://digital.nhs.uk/

Since the WannaCry incident, NHS Digital has publicly stated that its reinforced cybersecurity posture has been instrumental in preventing subsequent attacks of a similar scale. This is evident in their ability to avoid significant disruptions from other ransomware strains that have emerged since. The organisation's proactive stance, including investments in new technologies and fostering a security-first mindset among employees, has been critical in protecting sensitive patient data and ensuring continuity of care.

Barclays Bank[15][16]

Barclays Bank has consistently been at the forefront of integrating cybersecurity into its operational and corporate culture. Recognising the significant threat posed by cyber-attacks, particularly those targeting financial institutions, Barclays has made substantial investments in technology and employee training to safeguard against potential incidents.

Barclays has publicly highlighted the success of its cybersecurity culture in reducing phishing attacks and other social engineering threats. The

---

[15] Barclays Bank. (2019). *Cybersecurity: Protecting our customers in a digital age*. Retrieved from https://www.barclays.com

[16] Financial Conduct Authority. (2018). *Cyber resilience: The evolution of cybersecurity in UK financial services*. Retrieved from https://www.fca.org.uk/

bank's strategy includes mandatory cybersecurity training for all employees, regular phishing simulations, and a strong emphasis on reporting suspicious activity. These efforts have created a security-conscious workforce capable of recognising and responding to potential threats before they escalate.

In several instances, Barclays has reported that its enhanced cybersecurity culture directly prevented incidents that could have led to significant financial and reputational damage. The bank's commitment to cybersecurity is also reflected in its partnerships with external cybersecurity firms and participation in industry-wide initiatives to improve overall resilience in the financial sector.

BT Group (British Telecom) [17] [18]

BT Group, one of the UK's leading telecommunications companies, has positioned itself as a cybersecurity leader within its operations and as a service provider to other organisations. Recognising the increasing sophistication of cyber threats, BT has implemented a robust cybersecurity strategy integrating advanced threat detection

---

[17] BT Group. (2020). *Cybersecurity: Staying ahead of the threats*. Retrieved from https://www.bt.com

[18] Computer Weekly. (2018). *BT's cybersecurity strategy pays off with proactive threat prevention*. Retrieved from https://www.computerweekly.com/

technologies, continuous monitoring, and a solid internal security culture.

BT has publicly shared instances where its cybersecurity measures have successfully identified and neutralised threats before they could impact operations. This includes preventing distributed denial-of-service (DDoS) attacks and other network-based threats that could have disrupted critical communications infrastructure. The company attributes its success to cutting-edge technology and a deeply ingrained security culture among its employees.

A key aspect of BT's approach is its focus on employee training and awareness. By ensuring that all employees, regardless of their role, understand the importance of cybersecurity and are equipped to identify potential threats, BT has created a resilient organisational culture that acts as a first line of defence against cyber incidents.

National Grid [19] [20]

National Grid, responsible for managing the UK's electricity and gas transmission networks, has placed a high priority on cybersecurity due to the critical nature of its infrastructure. In recent years, the organisation has undertaken significant efforts to enhance its cybersecurity posture, acknowledging the increasing threats posed by cyber-attacks on national infrastructure.

National Grid's approach to cybersecurity is multifaceted. It involves implementing advanced technologies and strongly focusing on cultivating a cybersecurity-aware culture. This includes regular cybersecurity drills, incident response simulations, and ongoing training programs to keep all employees vigilant and informed about the latest threats.

Publicly, National Grid has credited these efforts with preventing potential cyber incidents that could have severely affected the UK's energy supply. By integrating cybersecurity into its overall risk management strategy, National Grid has successfully mitigated threats and maintained the integrity of its operations.

---

[19] National Grid. (2020). *Ensuring cybersecurity across our critical infrastructure*. Retrieved from https://www.nationalgrid.com

[20] Energy UK. (2019). *Cyber resilience in the UK energy sector: A collaborative approach*. Retrieved from https://www.energy-uk.org.uk/

Tesco Bank [21] [22]

Tesco Bank, part of the UK-based retail giant Tesco, faced a significant cyber-attack in 2016, which resulted in the theft of funds from customer accounts. In response to this incident, Tesco Bank implemented a comprehensive overhaul of its cybersecurity practices, focusing on technological improvements and strengthening its internal cybersecurity culture.

The bank introduced more stringent security protocols, improved its incident detection and response capabilities, and launched extensive cybersecurity training programs for its employees. Tesco Bank has since highlighted these initiatives as key factors in preventing further incidents, with the strengthened cybersecurity culture playing a critical role in this success.

In various public statements and industry forums, Tesco Bank has emphasised the importance of a proactive approach to cybersecurity, noting that the changes made post-2016 have been instrumental in protecting customer data and maintaining trust. The bank's experience

---

[21] Tesco Bank. (2017). *Cybersecurity and the protection of our customers.* Retrieved from https://www.tescobank.com

[22] BBC News. (2016). *Tesco Bank hack: Cybersecurity overhaul and lessons learned.* Retrieved from https://www.bbc.co.uk/news/business

underscores the value of learning from past incidents and continuously evolving cybersecurity practices to address new and emerging threats.

These examples demonstrate that a strong cybersecurity culture, characterised by vigilance, proactive measures, and continuous improvement, can significantly reduce the impact of cyber incidents.

Chapter 11

Key Insights and Future Trends

In this book, we've explored the complex landscape of security threats and culture's pivotal role in fortifying organisations against these ever-evolving challenges. Creating a security-conscious organisation involves implementing the latest technologies and nurturing an environment where every member is empowered and educated to act as a vigilant security steward. The path toward enhanced resilience is multifaceted, involving a concerted effort to understand the nuances of behavioural psychology, cultural dimensions, and the intrinsic human factors that influence security posture.

The synthesis of behavioural science with practical, actionable strategies has illuminated the pathway for leaders not only to anticipate future threats but to engineer a cultural transformation that embeds security into the very fabric of their organisations. As we look forward, the onus is on leaders to continue adapting, evolving, and fostering a culture of continuous improvement and openness, where the principles of a resilient security culture are applied and lived by every individual. This responsibility and influence of leaders is crucial in the journey towards a more secure future. The goal has always been to transcend mere compliance and reach a state where security is as natural and intrinsic as the mission and values that drive the organisation.

Let the insights and strategies outlined serve as a beacon, guiding the creation of more secure, vigilant, and resilient organisations that stand steadfast in the face of tomorrow's cyber threats. Embrace the journey ahead with determination and optimism, knowing that the cultural transformation you embark upon is a strategic advantage and a fundamental necessity in our interconnected digital world. With this mindset, we can genuinely begin to future-proof our organisations against the myriad of security challenges on the horizon. This journey is not just important; it's inspiring and motivating.

Summary of Key Insights

As we've explored throughout this book, creating a resilient entity is not merely about adopting the latest technologies but embedding a security-first mindset across all levels of the organisation.

The advent of modern security threats has underscored the importance of understanding the nuances of cyber, physical, and cyber-physical threats. Technology's impact on security is profound, introducing new vulnerabilities while simultaneously offering innovative solutions. In this dynamic environment, staying ahead means being proactive, not reactive. Leaders must balance adopting emerging technologies with the potential security implications they entail.

Moreover, the human factor plays an integral role in the security equation. Recognising and mitigating behavioural risks is essential for building a secure organisation. This entails a deep dive into the psychology of security vulnerabilities, addressing how human behaviour can both pose a risk and serve as a line of defence against threats.

Exploring cultural dimensions has illuminated how cultural values shape perceptions of security and risk. A one-size-fits-all approach to security is ineffective. Instead, customised strategies that reflect the unique cultural contexts of an organisation's global footprint are required. This cultural sensitivity is critical in formulating and implementing security policies that employees across diverse geographies embrace.

At the heart of a robust security culture are principles and strategies that foster resilience. Educational initiatives and engaging employees play a crucial role in mindset change, while leadership is tasked with embodying and promoting this culture of security awareness. The role of leaders in driving cultural change cannot be overstated - training and commitment at the leadership level are indispensable for cultivating a pervasive security consciousness.

Applying behavioural science to enact security behaviour change represents a powerful lever. Designing interventions that resonate with employees and integrating technology as an enabler of cultural initiatives has shown promise. Such strategies support the embedding of security practices and facilitate their measurement and continuous improvement.

The global context of security practices adds another layer of complexity. From North America to Asia and from Europe to Africa, cultural diversity demands tailored approaches to security. Understanding these regional nuances is paramount in crafting a security strategy that is both globally coherent and locally applicable.

Security Champions emerge as vital agents of change within this framework. Identifying, selecting, and empowering these individuals within various departments can significantly amplify the reach and impact of security initiatives. Providing them with the necessary training and resources is fundamental to their success in fostering a security-aware culture.

Looking towards the future, anticipating threats, and devising scalable, adaptable security strategies are crucial to remaining resilient. This foresight and an ongoing commitment to cultural change position organisations to navigate the evolving security landscape effectively.

Integrating cultural change into security strategy is more than a tactical move - it's a strategic imperative. Evaluating the current cultural landscape regarding security, identifying barriers and facilitators, and employing culturally aware security strategies are steps that can't be overlooked. Monitoring cultural change and continuously refining security strategies through established feedback loops will ensure that efforts are both practical and enduring.

In conclusion, the journey towards creating a security-conscious organisation is ongoing. It requires diligence, foresight, and a commitment to culture change. By embracing these insights and strategies, leaders can fortify their organisations against the multifaceted threats of the modern world. The goal is not just to protect but to thrive in an environment where security is woven into the very fabric of the organisation's culture.

The insights provided herein serve as a blueprint for navigating the complexities of building a resilient security culture. This synthesis of understanding threats, leveraging technology, and fostering behavioural and cultural change offers a comprehensive strategy for any leader looking to enhance their organisation's security posture. It's an investment that pays dividends in safeguarding assets and building trust and enabling business continuity in an increasingly interconnected and digital world.

As we move forward, it's important to remember that security is not solely the domain of IT departments or security professionals. It's a collective responsibility that requires engagement, understanding, and action from every corner of the organisation. Organisations can transform security from a perceived constraint into a strategic advantage by cultivating a security-conscious culture. This transformation paves the way for survival and flourishing in the digital age.

Future Trends

As the cybersecurity landscape continues to evolve, driven by rapid technological advancements and increasingly sophisticated threats, the concept of security culture is gaining more prominence. The future of security culture is not merely about maintaining compliance or adhering to standard protocols; it is about fostering a deeply ingrained mindset where security becomes second nature to every employee, regardless of their role. This emerging vision is supported by cutting-edge research and forward-thinking approaches that shape how organisations will approach security in the years to come.

A critical development in this space is the growing recognition that security culture is not a one-size-fits-all solution. Each organisation must craft a culture that reflects its unique risks, industry challenges, and workforce dynamics. Research suggests that a tailored approach to security culture, one that considers the diverse backgrounds, values, and behaviours of employees, can lead to more effective outcomes. Rather than relying solely on prescriptive training and awareness programs, future strategies will emphasise a more contextualised understanding of how security behaviours manifest within specific organisational ecosystems.

The shift towards a more human-centric approach to security is also gaining traction. The notion of 'human risk management' is becoming a cornerstone of security culture development. This approach emphasises understanding the psychological, social, and behavioural factors influencing how employees perceive and respond to security risks. Research in this area highlights the importance of using behavioural science techniques, such as nudging and social influence, to gently steer individuals toward more secure practices. By understanding the cognitive biases and heuristics that drive decision-making, organisations can design interventions that align with natural human tendencies, making secure behaviour the path of least resistance.

The future of security culture will also see a closer alignment with organisational values and overall business goals. As businesses become more digitally integrated, there is a growing need for security to be seen not as a barrier to innovation but as an enabler of business agility and resilience. A forward-thinking security culture will embed security considerations into the fabric of business operations, from product development to customer engagement. This will involve fostering cross-functional collaboration, where security is part of the conversation from the outset rather than an afterthought.

Moreover, the role of leadership in shaping the future of security culture cannot be overstated. Leaders must model the behaviours they wish to see in their employees, demonstrating a commitment to security beyond compliance. Emerging research points to the critical influence of 'Security Champions'—individuals who serve as role models and advocates for security within different parts of the organisation. These champions are crucial in creating a security-conscious environment by fostering peer-to-peer learning and support, making security a shared responsibility across all levels.

Finally, technology will play a significant role in the evolution of security culture. The rise of artificial intelligence and machine learning offers new opportunities for creating adaptive and personalised security experiences. Future security culture initiatives will leverage data-driven insights to identify areas of vulnerability in real time, enabling more targeted interventions. Automated systems will help alleviate some cognitive load on employees by handling repetitive security tasks, allowing them to focus on more strategic security decisions. However, these technological advancements must be integrated thoughtfully, ensuring that they enhance rather than replace the human element of security culture.

In conclusion, the future direction of security culture is moving towards a more nuanced, human-centred, and integrated approach. Relying on static training programs or top-down policies will no longer be enough; the security culture of tomorrow will be dynamic, adaptable, and deeply embedded in every aspect of the organisation. By embracing these emerging trends and applying cutting-edge research, organisations can build a security culture that is resilient to today's threats and agile enough to face the challenges of tomorrow.

A Final Word

A security-conscious organisation hinges on a balanced approach to technology, human behaviour, and environmental culture. As we forge ahead, our success will be measured by the security breaches we prevent and the culture we nurture. This endeavour is both a challenge and an opportunity - an invitation to lead, innovate, and transform in pursuing a more secure tomorrow.

Let this be a call to action. The path ahead will require resolve, creativity, and collaboration. But with a steadfast commitment to enhancing security awareness and behaviours at every level of our organisations, we can aspire to not just navigate but thrive in the face of the evolving security landscape.

All the best in your endeavours.

Beyond this book

The field of culture and behavioural change is continually advancing with fresh theories, models, and practices. To stay current on how these can be applied within the cybersecurity domain and access the latest insights, whitepapers, guides, and tools for fostering a cybersecurity culture, visit our website, **Beyond the Firewall**, at www.BuildASecurityCulture.com.

www.ingramcontent.com/pod-product-compliance
Lightning Source LLC
Chambersburg PA
CBHW062212220526
45471CB00009B/3169